SOCIETY FOR OLD TESTAMENT STUDY

MONOGRAPH SERIES

General Editor: R. E. Clements

6

AMOS'S ORACLES AGAINST THE NATIONS

A study of Amos 1.3–2.5

Other books in the series:

R. N. Whybray: *The Heavenly Counsellor in Isaiah xl 13–14: A study of the sources of the theology of Deutero-Isaiah.*

Joseph Blenkinsopp: *Gibeon and Israel: The role of Gibeon and the Gibeonites in the political and religious history of early Israel.*

Patrick H. Vaughan: *The meaning of 'Bāmâ' in the Old Testament: A study of etymological, textual and archaeological evidence.*

D. W. Gooding: *Relics of Ancient Exegesis: A study of the miscellanies in 3 Reigns 2.*

G. I. Davies: *The Way of the Wilderness: A study of the Wilderness Itineraries in the Old Testament.*

Amos's Oracles against the Nations

A study of Amos 1.3–2.5

JOHN BARTON

CAMBRIDGE UNIVERSITY PRESS

CAMBRIDGE
LONDON · NEW YORK · NEW ROCHELLE
MELBOURNE · SYDNEY

Published by the Press Syndicate of the University of Cambridge
The Pitt Building, Trumpington Street, Cambridge CB2 1RP
32 East 57th Street, New York, NY 10022, USA
296 Beaconsfield Parade, Middle Park, Melbourne 3206, Australia

First published 1980

Printed in Great Britain at the
University Press, Cambridge

Library of Congress Cataloguing in Publication Data
Barton, John, 1948–
    Amos's oracles against the nations.
    (Society for Old Testament Study monograph series)
    Bibliography: p.
    Includes indexes.
1. Bible. O.T. Amos I,3–II,5 – Criticism, interpretation, etc. I. Title.
II. Series: Society for Old Testament Study. Monograph Series.
BS1585.2.B37   224'.8'06   78-67630
ISBN 0 521 22501 9

CONTENTS

PREFACE

This monograph is an expanded version of a chapter of my doctoral thesis 'The Relation of God to Ethics in the Eighth Century Prophets', submitted to the University of Oxford in 1974. My thanks are due in the first place to Canon J. A. Baker, who supervised the research on which it rested. I should also like to record my gratitude to Dr R. E. Clements who, as Editor, accepted this work for the Monograph Series, and who also made helpful comments and suggestions; to the Society for Old Testament Study and the Board of Management of the Pusey and Ellerton Fund, who contributed generously to the cost of publication; and to the staff of Cambridge University Press, and especially Mr Eric Van Tassel, who made many helpful suggestions for improvements in style and presentation. The greater part of my research was done in the Bodleian Library, and I am particularly grateful to the staff of the Radcliffe Camera for their friendly efficiency; while I owe a debt to many colleagues and pupils in Oxford for encouragement, criticism, and advice.

To three people I owe debts of a different kind: to my wife Mary, for unfailing support throughout the time that this monograph has been in preparation; and to my parents, to whom I dedicate it, for their encouragement and practical help during the years of research which, without their generosity and kindness, would have led nowhere.

St Cross College, Oxford   J.B.
September 1979

ABBREVIATIONS

AfO	*Archiv für Orientforschung*
ANET	*Ancient Near Eastern Texts relating to the Old Testament,* ed. J. B. Pritchard, 2nd edn, Princeton 1955
ARMT	Archives Royales de Mari:
	vol. I: G. Dossin (ed.), *Correspondance de Šamši-Addu*, Paris 1946
	vol. II: C. F. Jean (ed.), *Lettres diverses*, Paris 1941
	vol. V: G. Dossin (ed.), *Correspondance de Iašmaḫ-Addu*, Paris 1946
	vol. VI: J. R. Kupper (ed.), *Correspondance de Baḫdi-Lim*, Paris 1953
ATD	Das Alte Testament Deutsch, ed. A. Weiser, Göttingen
AThR	*Anglican Theological Review*
BASOR	*Bulletin of the American Schools of Oriental Research*
BHS	Biblia Hebraica Stuttgartensia
BK	Biblischer Kommentar, ed. M. Noth and H. W. Wolff, Neukirchen
BoTU	*Die Boghazköi-Texte in Umschrift*, ed. E. Forrer, WVDOG 41 and 42, Leipzig 1922 and 1926
BWANT	Beiträge zur Wissenschaft vom Alten und Neuen Testament, Leipzig
BZAW	Beihefte zur *Zeitschrift für die alttestamentliche Wissenschaft*, Berlin
CBQ	*Catholic Bible Quarterly*
CH	Codex Hammurabi
EA	J. Knudtzon, *Die El-Amarna Tafeln*, Leipzig 1907–8
EvTh	*Evangelische Theologie*
HAT	Handbuch zum Alten Testament, ed. O. Eissfeldt, Tübingen
HUCA	*Hebrew Union College Annual*
IB	Interpreter's Bible
ICC	International Critical Commentary, Edinburgh

IEJ	*Israel Exploration Journal*
JB	Jerusalem Bible
JBL	*Journal of Biblical Literature*
JTS	*Journal of Theological Studies*
KAI	H. Donner and W. Röllig, *Kanaanäische und aramäische Inschriften*, 2nd edn, Wiesbaden 1966
KBo	*Keilsschrifttexte aus Boghazköi*, ed. H. H. Figulla *et al.*, WVDOG 30, 36, 68, 72, 78, 79, 82, 86 and 90, Leipzig 1916-
KUB	*Keilschrifturkunden aus Boghazköi*, 28 vols., Berlin 1921–44
LXX	Septuagint
MT	Massoretic Text
MVAG	Mitteilungen der vorderasiatisch-ägyptischen Gesellschaft, Leipzig
NEB	The New English Bible
OS	*Oudtestamentische Studiën*
OTL	Old Testament Library, London
PEQ	*Palestine Exploration Quarterly*
PJB	*Palästinajahrbuch des deutschen evangelischen Instituts für Altertumswissenschaft des Heiligen Landes zu Jerusalem*
RV	Revised Version
SBTh	Studies in Biblical Theology, London
STh	*Studia Theologica*, Lund
VT	*Vetus Testamentum*
VTE	D. J. Wiseman, 'The Vassal Treaties of Esarhaddon', *Iraq* 20 (1958)
VTS	Supplements to *Vetus Testamentum*
WMANT	Wissenschaftliche Monographien zum Alten und Neuen Testament, Neukirchen
WVDOG	Wissenschaftliche Veröffentlichungen der deutschen Orientgesellschaft, Leipzig
ZAW	*Zeitschrift für die alttestamentliche Wissenschaft*
ZDPV	*Zeitschrift des deutschen Palästina-Vereins*
ZThK	*Zeitschrift für Theologie und Kirche*

INTRODUCTION

Why does the book of Amos begin with a series of oracles against Israel's neighbours, and only then turn to denounce the prophet's own people? Is it a remnant of an older way of prophecy, the way of Balaam and of the four hundred prophets of Ahab, reinforcing a narrow nationalism with a word of power; is it the expression of a radically new insight, the discovery, made for the first time in the eighth century, that not just Israel but all nations, whatever their prestige and vaunted might, stood under the judgment of Yahweh; or is it a literary device, designed to throw the urbane and comfortable sins of Israel into high relief by seeing them against the background of the apparently grosser outrages perpetrated by barbarian nations, whom the prophet's complacent hearers would be only too ready to condemn, not noticing until too late that in condemning them they were condemning themselves? All of these explanations are possible, none is self-evidently right, and combinations of them are conceivable. Another question which might be asked, however, adds considerably to the difficulty of choosing between them. Why does Amos think that these other nations *are* accountable for their atrocities – wherein does their particular atrociousness lie? Is it that Yahweh, Israel's lawgiver and judge, has laid down laws which even foreign nations must obey – that extension of Yahweh's moral sphere of influence with which the eighth-century prophets used commonly to be credited? Is Amos drawing some kind of analogy between Israel's known obligation to her God and one supposed to be incumbent on foreigners, perhaps especially on those foreigners who belong to the immediate world of Palestinian politics, who had formed the components of David's empire? Or should we see the prophet's evident sense of moral outrage as indicating a belief in moral principles held to be obvious to all right-minded men, or even as evidence that actual conventions about the conduct of war and international relations existed in the Palestine of Amos's day, to which he might tacitly appeal? Here, then, is a second range of questions which have attracted rather less attention than the first, but which are equally important to an understanding of Amos's

1

thought; and unless both sets of questions are tackled together, we are unlikely to make much progress in forming a coherent interpretation of the prophet and his book.

The purpose of this study is to examine the oracles against the nations in the first two chapters of Amos, in an attempt to discover exactly what point the prophet was making when he condemned Israel's neighbours for atrocities in war, and did so in this particular literary form. It will be suggested that he was appealing to a kind of conventional or customary law about international conduct which he at least believed to be self-evidently right, and which he thought he could count on his audience's familiarity with and acquiescence in. We shall further maintain that this has important consequences for understanding Amos's whole approach to ethics, since at a crucial place in his message he sees moral conduct as a matter of conformity to a human convention held to be obviously universal, rather than to the overt or explicit demands of God: in other words, ethics in Amos is not simply a question of theonomy, as it is quite widely thought to be. We shall also be concerned with other instances of conventional morality, inside and outside Israel, and with other problems about Amos, his book and his prophetic role, which our interpretation of chapters 1-2 raises.

CHAPTER 1

Rather than beginning with a lengthy survey of the state of the question, I propose in this chapter to outline the interpretation of Amos's oracles against the nations which it will be the task of the rest of this study to justify. I shall set it out as a continuous argument, and then indicate the points at which it seems specially to stand in need of justification. In the chapters that follow each of these will be taken up and discussed against the background of recent work.

Apart from the oracles of Balaam, Amos 1.3-2.5 constitutes the earliest example in the Old Testament of a genre that was to become a regular feature of prophetic books, the cycle of oracles against foreign nations. These oracles, with the probable exception of those on Judah, Edom, and Tyre, are the work of the prophet Amos himself, and are probably among his own earliest oracles. Unlike many prophetic oracles they are neither old material adapted by the prophet for a new purpose, nor short, individual sayings collected by an editor, but are a free composition which formed from the beginning a continuous whole. The purpose of the oracles on the nations is to lead up to the oracle on Israel in 2.6ff; though it is no longer clear where this ends, it was intended by the prophet as the climax to the whole cycle, and the overall effect is to produce surprise and horror in the intended audience. This is achieved by a rhetorical trick similar to that found in Nathan's parable (II Samuel 12), Isaiah's Song of the Vineyard (Isaiah 5), and Amos's own visions in Amos 7. The prophet begins by condemning the surrounding nations for atrocities committed during military campaigns, and by mentioning well-known incidents he ensures that his hearers will experience a sense of moral outrage – which indeed he fully shares himself: the condemnations are meant with full seriousness, and might well have been felt by his audience to be a proper expression of his prophetic vocation. Having won the people's sympathy and agreement, he rounds on them by proclaiming judgment on Israel, too. This technique has two obvious advantages. First, it ensures that the prophet's word of doom will be heard, since he has gained his audience's attention by flatter-ing their feelings of superiority and their natural xenophobia. Secondly, it makes it much harder for them to exculpate themselves or dismiss the prophet's message as mere raving, since they have implicitly conceded that sin and judgment are rightly linked, by their approval of what has gone before. (For our purposes it matters little whether we think of the audience as literally present – say at a festal gathering, as some suggest – or as pre-sent only to the prophet's imagination, and the oracles as a literary com-position.)

For Amos to have supposed that this technique would be successful, he must have held the following beliefs about his intended audience's mentality:

(1) That they thought manifest evil-doing both deserved and would receive divine punishment.
(2) That they regarded the nations condemned as moral agents, i.e. as answerable for their actions, particularly in the conduct of war.
(3) That they thought Israel had a specially privileged position which indemnified her against divine judgment.
(4) That they did not expect prophets to proclaim judgment on Israel.
(5) That they did not regard the kind of sins of which Amos accuses Israel as at all comparable in gravity with atrocities in war.
(6) That it was more obvious to them that the nations had moral obli-gations towards each other than that Israelites had moral obliga-tions among themselves.

It cannot be shown that any of these assumptions was in fact correct; but it can be shown that unless Amos thought they were, his tactics in con-structing chapters 1 and 2 were unintelligent. For if he did not believe (1) or (2), he could not expect the people to react with approval to his con-demnation of the nations; if he did not believe (3) or (4), he could hardly expect to surprise them with the oracle against Israel; if he did not believe (5), then the Israel oracle could not be expected to produce any *more* sur-prise than the others; while unless he believed (6), his chosen literary form would be a piece of sheer bathos. For so far from the Israel oracle coming as a surprise, it would be the only part of the cycle that would occasion none. Any successful didactic technique must begin from the better known and move on to the less well known: and if the moral obligation owed by the nations is a novelty, whereas that owed by Israel is common ground, then the whole cycle is very incompetently put together, building down to a spectacular anti-climax.

It might be thought that we should add a seventh assumption:

(7) That the people expected prophets to denounce foreign nations.

– for otherwise would they not have been surprised at Amos's foreign oracles, and thus spoiled for the extra surprise of the Israel oracle? But this is an unnecessary supposition. Certainly, it cannot have been thought strange that anyone should denounce foreigners; but need the people have thought of this as a specially prophetic activity? One might guess that anyone was welcome to speak out against the crimes of aliens. We may not validly deduce that it was regarded as part of a prophet's role to do so; though of course this might be true in fact, and demonstrable on other grounds.

If this analysis is correct, then certain conclusions may be drawn about the moral norms appealed to in the oracles against the nations, and also about the theological importance of Amos. These are:

(1) Amos did not think that he was being original in claiming that foreign nations were subject to certain moral obligations, at least in their international relations, nor in claiming that God would punish infringements of them. In this he was merely echoing what he took to be popular belief and sentiment. Consequently no interpretation of the prophet can be correct which regards him as an innovator in this respect.

(2) Since Amos thus appeals to a supposed consensus so far as the conduct of war by the nations is concerned, it is unlikely that we should be able to discover any underlying rationale for such moral norms. In particular it is improbable that they were seen by the prophet's audience as deeply theological, or as deriving from divine laws; rather they seem best classified as customary law or convention, or even a kind of commonsense morality: after all, they need reflect no more than the feeling that there ought to be a convention banning certain kinds of conduct, even where no convention in fact exists. It would be interesting to compare these with the norms of conduct Amos supposes to be binding within Israel. *Prima facie* there is no reason to suppose that the prophet had any overall 'theory' of ethical obligation, such as that it derived from the covenant relationship, from the universal rule of God, or from the order of nature. The existence of merely conventional morality in the Old Testament has not been much explored, and so we may hope to break a little fresh ground. Further, since the area of conduct involved is that of international relations, especially in warfare, it will be interesting to explore the question whether any conventions did in fact exist on this subject, either inside Israel or elsewhere in the ancient Near East: and here we hope to provide a convenient summary of some material not previously collected together.

(3) Although we have been careful throughout to say that Amos

supposed his hearers to hold certain beliefs, rather than that they did in fact hold them, it would be odd if he were badly mistaken in his assumptions. What a man takes for granted in arguing with opponents, what he never feels it necessary to prove, is generally the best evidence for the popular beliefs of his day precisely because it is not being insisted upon.[1] It is therefore probable that the first six points outlined above do fairly represent the beliefs of a good many eighth-century Israelites, though we should of course reckon with the possibility that Amos deliberately exaggerates their obtuseness, just as St Paul would widely be held to exaggerate the heterodoxy of teachers against whom he warns his converts. We can therefore form some idea of popular notions about morality, prophecy, and divine judgment, and also about the relationship of Yahweh and Israel. And in the light of this it will make sense to raise the perennial question about the distinctiveness of classical prophecy, attempting to pinpoint the 'new thing' in the preaching of Amos. Our conclusion must be that Amos is not original in proclaiming that sin calls down divine judgment, nor in seeing that Israel had moral obligations to Yahweh, but chiefly in two things:

(i) in regarding social morality as a decisive area of conduct, just as important for the continuance of Yahweh's favour as the avoidance of much crasser and more 'obvious' crimes; and

(ii) in arguing with the people so as to show that their conduct is unreasonable and their complacency foolish and shortsighted. It is presupposed by the use of the 'surprise' technique and also by the insistence on giving reasons for Yahweh's judgment that the people are at least in principle open to rational persuasion, even if in practice they have succeeded in blinding their own eyes and are now too far gone to recover – the problem which both Isaiah and Ezekiel were later to face and discuss. This emphasis on rationality in Amos, indeed, aligns him very clearly with Isaiah, and our discussion is related to recent attempts to trace 'wisdom influence' on his book – though we shall not try to define the point in precisely that way.

In the chapters that follow we shall discuss in detail what may be regarded as the 'sensitive' areas of this line of interpretation. Since our argument is that the thought of Amos himself may be detected behind the oracles in chapters 1 and 2, we shall devote a chapter to examining the provenance of these oracles, considering a number of recent arguments which try to show that the prophet or his editor is simply taking over an older collection, possibly cultic in origin. In chapter 3 we turn to examine the oracles for authenticity, attempting to decide on literary and historical grounds whether any of them need to be regarded as later additions to Amos. These two chapters together may be seen as making a case for at least a core of the oracles against the nations as the work of the prophet himself, and as an attempt to make their simple exegesis clear. This leads us, in chapter 4, to ask whether the historical circumstances of the atrocities they condemn can be established, and we conclude that, although it is fair to think that all of the events will have been readily identifiable to the prophet's audience, there is not enough evidence for us to identify them positively. This in turn rules out interpretations of the oracles which absolutely require that they refer either to very remote or very recent events. Chapter 5 looks in more detail at the case for seeing an effect of climax in the juxtaposition of oracles against foreign nations and against Israel, suggesting that this is both inherently probable and consonant with what we know of the prophet's method from other parts of his book. Finally in chapter 6 we try to show that it is better to see the underlying ethical approach in these oracles as an appeal to (at least supposedly) international norms of conduct than to tie them down to any covenant- or Israel-centred ethic. An appendix surveys a little of the evidence for the existence of such international conventions on war and other matters in Israel and among her neighbours: this is intended to show that the kind of interpretation we have proposed is not historically impossible, and to illustrate it with some interesting parallels, but it is not supposed to be in any way probative.

CHAPTER 2

Do the first two chapters of Amos represent a new departure in Israelite prophecy, or are they part of a long-established tradition? There seems to be something like a consensus in recent writings on the prophets that Amos is here drawing on a tradition already very old by his time, and perhaps even on old oracles against the nations which he simply selected because they suited his purpose. Thus R. E. Clements, in his recent study *Prophecy and Tradition*:

> In the earliest literary collection of such prophecies in Amos 1.3–2.6 there are strong indications that the form of such oracles, the style of their presentation, and perhaps also the type of motive adduced for such threats, were already well-established features of prophetic preaching.[1]

The main reasons for such a judgment were summarised by N. K. Gottwald's detailed study *All the Kingdoms of the Earth*[2] and developed by J. H. Hayes in an article four years later,[3] though both build on a great deal of previous discussion. The arguments may be reduced to three main types, all in fact closely connected.

1. Hayes suggests that prophetic oracles against the nations have their roots in 'the tradition of Holy War', and are closely related to taunts and challenges to battle.[4] But whereas a taunt is essentially directed against an individual, and is specially appropriate in cases of single combat,[5] the prophetic oracle is primarily directed against the whole hostile nation. The earliest example of this form in the Old Testament is probably Numbers 21.27–30, the taunt-song against Heshbon, which Gottwald suggests may go back to a pre-Israelite poem, perhaps from the Amorite period.[6] Cases of the actual use of the second-person form in time of war are not common in the Old Testament, but it passes into the prophetic tradition and appears in classic form in Isaiah 10 and 14, and Ezekiel 27 and 28. But the commonest form of prophecy relating to war is reached when the direct second-person address to the enemy[7] is aban-

doned in favour of an assurance given to the prophet's own nation or its ruler, referring to the enemy in the third person, and denouncing him. This form reaches its first literary expression in Israel in the oracles of Balaam, which recent studies have suggested go back at least to the period of the United Monarchy and are probably based on pre-monarchic poems.[8] But that it was one function of a prophet to deliver such oracles is plain, according to Hayes, from I Samuel 15.2-3, I Kings 20.26-30, and II Kings 13.17b - and we might add I Kings 22. Several commentators have suggested that Isaiah's oracles in 7.3-9 can be understood against this background as an 'oracle of assurance to the king in time of battle' (*Kriegsansprache*);[9] and their common use of such forms has been one of the factors inclining Old Testament scholars to see affinities between Israelite prophets and the ecstatics of the Mari letters.[10]

But even supposing all this to be right, its relevance to Amos's oracles against the nations must surely be judged very slender. The theory of dependence on such a prophetic tradition can be dismissed on quite general grounds: we can appeal to Fohrer's standard objection[11] that the context in which a form originates tells us very little about its use in any given case, especially when that use is manifestly literary; we might also argue that Israel was not at war with any of the nations in question, and even in theory could scarcely have been at war with all of them at once.[12] Yet against this it might still be held that Amos was taking an old tradition and transforming it for his own purposes. But we can surely go further and maintain that the 'tradition of Holy War' (supposing such a 'tradition' to have existed) has played no part at all in shaping these oracles. Not only is Israel not in fact at war with the nations mentioned: their attitude to Israel is in several cases not the point at issue anyway, as is made specially clear in the oracle against Moab (2.1).[13] Amos is neither encouraging his people to fight in assurance of victory, nor encouraging them to remain passive in expectation of Yahweh's deliverance. He is not, indeed, encouraging them at all; but in view of the oracle on Israel our point is that he is not even pretending to encourage them. We shall have later to examine the actual incidents referred to, and shall suggest that at least some of them may have taken place during comparatively recent attacks on Israel by the nations concerned; but it is not plausible to suppose that Amos, prophesying under Jeroboam II, saw Israel threatened and hemmed in on all sides.[14] Common sense tends rather against the derivation of these oracles from the background of 'Holy War'.

We may add as a rider to this an interesting observation made by Clements on prophetic oracles against the nations in general. He points out that the feature of Israel's enemies most commonly condemned by the prophets is their pride or *hybris* towards Yahweh; thus in Isaiah 14.12ff, 16.6, 23.6-12; Jeremiah 48.28-33; Ezekiel 28.1ff, 31.1ff, 32.1ff, 32.12ff.[15] Now in most of these cases the most likely reason for such a charge would seem to be the wish to suggest that the nation in question has failed to subordinate itself to Yahweh by accepting the privileged position of Israel, and instead has set itself up as God, thinking to put down Yahweh's chosen people. A case could reasonably (I think not compellingly) be made for seeing this particular charge as a lineal descendant of the taunt before battle: compare David's exchanges with Goliath in I Samuel 17.43-7. But Amos's oracles make no mention of *hybris*; they concentrate on moral outrages committed by one nation against another. Thus the similarity between Amos 1-2 and other prophetic oracles against the nations is not very great, and Hayes's interesting suggestion cannot readily be made to cover the case of Amos.

So much can be said even on the supposition that Hayes's general thesis is correct. But Clements[16] adduces powerful arguments that suggest that it is not. As he points out, it is hardly surprising that oracles on the downfall of foreign nations should use military expressions and be similar to propaganda against an enemy: no form-critical explanation is necessary. We may also note a further weakness in Hayes's case. This is that the execration or taunt in the second person is formally quite distinct from the *Kriegsansprache* speaking of the enemy in the third person, and the development of the two should be considered separately. Now where the taunt does appear in prophetic oracles against the nations, it is most often in the form of a taunt-*song*, which is generally held to owe more to the funeral lament than to anything connected with the conduct of war. And the third-person references in the prophets are only occasionally (as in Isaiah 7) cast in the *Kriegsansprache* form anyway; in most cases they have no relation to any decision on the part of the Israelite king about whether or not to fight, and in many cases are directed towards nations with which Israel is in any case not at war. Hayes's theory gains its plausibility from lumping all 'oracles on the nations' together, and mixing form-critical considerations with observations about content. It does not really illuminate the complex picture presented by classical prophecy.

2. Hayes's second point (really a very closely related one, in view of the cultic associations of 'Holy War') is that another *Sitz im Leben* for oracles against foreign nations may be found in cultic ceremonies of lamentation, as attested by the existence of communal laments in the Psalter and elsewhere. He cites Psalms 20, 21 and 60; Lamentations 4.21-2; and II Kings 18.13-19.37. The transition from lamentation about military defeat (or petition for aid) to thanksgiving for either promised or actual deliverance

has long been acknowledged as a common feature of communal laments,[17] and form-critics have proposed various explanations: most commonly, that a cult-prophet intervened between the two halves to give an oracle of assurance, perhaps by denouncing in Yahweh's name the enemies at whose hands the people were suffering.[18] Indeed this could very well be one *Sitz im Leben* for the *Kriegsansprache* just discussed. In Psalm 20 the prophet's words are not recorded,[19] but Psalm 60 may perhaps provide what we are looking for in verses 6-8.[20] This is of particular interest for us since the nations it names – Moab, Edom and Philistia – also occur in Amos 1 and 2, and it looks very much as though such a psalm could be the model for Amos's oracles.

The idea that Amos modelled his oracles on some kind of prophetic liturgy of denunciation designed to bring victory to the armies of Israel has in fact a respectable history in the study of the prophet. Its most persuasive advocate was Würthwein, in his 'Amosstudien'.[21] According to him, Amos was originally a conventional cult-prophet, who foretold *Heil* for Israel in accordance with his traditional role. It is to this period of his life that the two visions 7.1-3 and 7.4-6 belong; only later did Amos become convinced that Yahweh's intentions were now hostile towards Israel, and he then added 7.7-9. Similarly, in 1.2-2.3, the *Heilsnabi* uses the traditional form of doom on his people's enemies, thus implying prosperity for Israel: it was only at a later date that he came to see that Israel, by her transgression of the covenant with Yahweh, was in even worse case than her enemies, and added 2.6-16.

A number of objections arise on points of detail. Against Würthwein, few commentators would now accept the designation of Amos as a converted *Heilsnabi*, so that the most we might salvage from his theory would be that Amos used the form of oracles on the nations as if he were such a prophet, for dramatic effect. But it is not altogether obvious that it was a peculiarly prophetic function to pronounce such oracles in any case: Begrich's article already cited (note 20) suggests the priest as a likelier candidate, and of course it is hard to identify the intended speaker in Psalm 60.6-8, and still more in Psalm 20, where even his words have dropped out! In the case of individual laments and petitions almost our only evidence is I Samuel 1 and 2, where it is the priest who delivers the assurance of God's favour; in II Kings 18.13-19.37, Hayes's example, the prophet Isaiah is consulted, but does not speak during a cultic ceremony, and here in any case the oracle in 19.21-8 seems to many most likely to be post-exilic.[22] More serious, it seems to me, is an objection which again depends on the content of the oracles, and which therefore necessarily anticipates some later discussion: that Amos 1 and 2 is not concerned, as is Psalm 60, with the possibility of Israel avenging herself, by God's help, on the nations who have oppressed her, but with the fact that God will himself find means to avenge atrocities not necessarily directed against Israel. Once again, therefore, Amos is not even parodying a stock form of oracle: these oracles are not related except very superficially to prophetic or priestly utterances during lamentations in times of national crisis.

3. The third line of approach supported by Hayes and Gottwald also sees prophecies against the nations within a cultic setting, but attempts to broaden the area of interest considerably and to think in terms of a feature common to many cultic celebrations, not just to services of national lamentation. Würthwein's subsequent article on the prophetic *Gerichtsrede* also worked along these lines.[23] Basic to this interpretation is the belief that a prophet's role was understood to be that of bringing salvation to his people not just by denouncing Israel's current enemies[24] but by a general and systematic execration of 'foreigners'; and that this was closely linked with the notion of Yahweh's covenant with Israel, and probably took place during a covenant festival – very likely that much-overworked feast, Tabernacles. Although cult prophecy does not now arouse the enthusiasm it once did, and many commentators regard any direct connection of the eighth-century prophets with the cult as unlikely, despite Reventlow's continued reconstructions,[25] it is still quite widely held that the prophetic oracles on the nations are a use of this *genre*, not a new creation by Amos and his successors; and so the theory must be examined so far as it relates to Amos 1 and 2. Its most popular form derives from Bentzen's attempt to link Amos 1 and 2 with the pattern of Egyptian execration texts.[26] This is still highly influential, and is accepted by both Hayes and Gottwald. Bentzen, it should be noted, maintains not that Amos was familiar with any execration texts, but that the pattern of his oracles entitles us to argue to a similar form and hence a similar *Sitz im Leben* in the Israelite cult. The execration texts, he says, call down curses on the enemies of Pharaoh in a fixed order, viz. southern nations – northern nations – western nations – individual Egyptians. The order in Amos is northeast (Aram) – southwest (Philistia) – northwest (Phoenicia) – southeast (Edom, Ammon, Moab) – Judah, Israel. Certainly there is a resemblance of form here sufficient to make one think of a common pattern – though it would be upset if, as can reasonably be argued, some of these oracles should be deleted.[27] But as M. Weiss has argued,[28] this 'common pattern' does not prove very much; for

(a) *all* Egyptian documents follow the order south–north–west, not just the execration texts,[29] and

(b) the order in Amos, if one ignores the fact that intermediate points of the compass are involved, is *not* south–north, but north–south, or perhaps east–west–north.

He further shows that one cannot bolster up the 'common pattern' by drawing on other prophetic oracles, as Fohrer does,[30] since no agreed geographical order can be extracted from them; compare

Ezek. 25–6: Ammon, Moab, Edom, Philistia, Tyre;
Jer. 27.3:   Edom, Moab, Ammon, Tyre, Sidon;
Zeph. 2:   Philistia, Moab, Ammon, Ethiopia, Assyria.

Weiss thinks that the reason for the Egyptian order is an orientation to the south (the source of the Nile) as the cardinal point.[31] One cannot be certain in what order if any the men of Amos's day in Israel boxed the compass, but Weiss argues, I think persuasively, that at any rate the east–west axis was primary rather than the north–south: this may be supported by noting that the west is called אָחוֹר, and the south יָמִין, suggesting a man facing east, and is confirmed by the order in Psalms 75.6 and 107.3.

If this is correct, then Amos differs from the execration texts in using an order different from that generally prevailing in his own culture. The simplest solution seems to be that the order is more or less arbitrary, or that other considerations than geography have dictated it.

One of the consequences of Bentzen's view, if accepted, is to eliminate any element of surprise in the Israel oracle.[32] The inclusion of Israel in the oracles is not to be seen as a surprise sprung by the prophet, who has lulled the people into expecting only good things for themselves when all the nations around them have been condemned; rather, it is the natural conclusion of a series of execrations, and it is surprising only in that, unlike its Egyptian models, it attacks the entire people instead of just the overt criminals among them, and threatens doom to them all. Wolff's recent commentary[33] seems to me, however, to dispose of this argument once and for all, going further than Weiss and in fact sharply challenging the whole cultic basis for these oracles. He argues that, even setting aside the geographical question, the execration texts are very remote from Amos 1 and 2. Thus:

(1) The Egyptian texts are in general mere lists of names, and exhibit nothing comparable to the structure of Amos 1 and 2.
(2) It is not really plausible that all the crimes concerned are against Israel, as those in the execration texts are against Egypt.
(3) The comprehensive threat to the whole Israelite nation is not just

a touch of originality, but undermines the whole basis of the comparison. In no case does an Egyptian curse turn against the Egyptian people as such.

(4) The Egyptian texts are magic formulae, designed to ensure the destruction of the nation's enemies: Amos's oracles are delivered in the name of Yahweh and betray no attempt to influence him against the nations. They are predictions, not curses.

In addition, Wolff notes that there is no evidence at all that ritual cursing of the kind envisaged formed part of the New Year festival, as Bentzen thinks, still less that it had to do with a special 'covenant festival' – Reventlow's view.[34]

But Wolff's arguments do not just demolish the evidence for thinking that Amos actually uttered these oracles at a cultic ceremony akin to the execration ceremonies of second-millennium Egypt; they remove any reason for thinking they are even a literary use of such a form. In short, the execration texts throw no light at all on Amos 1 and 2, and in no way support the argument that the prophet has drawn on an already existing tradition.

There are two other, more specific arguments, which claim to show that Amos was drawing on older traditions here.

(i) Gottwald suggests[35] that 'the historical allusions . . . seem to refer to a period as much as fifty to seventy-five years before the prophet'. In so far as this is an argument against these oracles' being a free creation by Amos, it will be dealt with below;[36] but Gottwald himself is far from confident about this: 'the historical argument is not decisive in itself, for it is always possible that Amos selected instances of national wrongdoing without respect to their modernity. The fact that they were committed years ago would not diminish his conviction that such wrong must be requited. It is when the historical argument is joined to the literary character of the oracles that the probability of a pre-Amosean prototype for the foreign oracles becomes very strong.'[37] So this is at best a supplementary argument, and we hope to have suggested that there is nothing for it to supplement.

(ii) Gottwald further suggests that the use of the words 'for three transgressions of . . . and for four' is anomalous, as in each case only one crime is mentioned (except in the Israel oracle). Of course this form usually suggests multiplicity rather than exact enumeration (compare NEB: 'for crime after crime of . . .') but it remains true that in other Old Testament examples – see especially Proverbs 30.18-19, 21-3, 24-8, 29-31; Ecclesiasticus 26.5 – the cases are in fact enumerated, and the fourth case often constitutes a 'punchline' (compare Ecclesiasticus 25.7-11). It is difficult, however, to see that this apparent lack of 'fit' proves that Amos is here selecting from already existing collections concerned with the crimes of the nations, as Gottwald claims.[38] Clements simply speaks of 'an element of traditional formalising',[39] which is certainly safer. Two counter-comments might be made. First, as Wolff suggests, it may be that Amos is simply giving the fourth, clinching example in each case - the last straw; there are several instances in the Old Testament where only the final $(x + 1)$ example is an actual crime - compare Ecclesiasticus 23.16-21, 26.28.[40] And secondly, if this is in fact a traditional form, all the indications are that x and $x + 1$ sayings are to be located in wisdom, whether by this we understand oral folk tradition or bureaucratic textbooks, and not in prophetic circles. This is a didactic device, not an oracular form.[41] Here then is a strong argument for Amos as an *innovator* within the prophetic succession, rather than a recipient of tradition.[42]

Our arguments in this chapter have all tended to underline Clements's conclusion:

> That any one sphere of Israel's life, the royal court, the cultus or the military organisation of the state with its inheritance of holy war ideology, formed the exclusive setting of the category of the oracles against foreign powers cannot be regarded as established. Rather we must regard these prophecies as a distinctive genre of their own which drew from many aspects of Israel's life.[43]

But we may add: Amos 1.3-2.5 is the earliest extant example of the genre. Of course we cannot prove that the prophet had no predecessors; but there is no reason to suppose that he had. If he was indeed using an earlier form, the conclusion nearest to hand is that he was adopting a popular proverbial form of speech, the numerical saying, and transforming it into prophecy by pre-fixing 'Thus saith the Lord'. If such forms had previously been used to condemn the sins of nations, that would help to suggest that its use by the prophet would ensure *rapport* with his audience; but I see no very compelling evidence that this is so. It is the content of the oracles against the nations, rather than their form, that wins the audience's approval. There is no need for any complicated form-critical hypothesis as to the oracle's *Sitz im Leben*; as Wolff comments, 'people never minded hearing their enemies being condemned'. [44]

CHAPTER 3

Our next task must be to identify more clearly what Amos is saying in these oracles. First we will set out a translation of the text, with brief textual notes; then give a simple exegesis; and finally proceed to a discussion of the oracles' authenticity.

Translation

Against the Aramaeans

Thus says the LORD: 'For three transgressions of Damascus and 1.3 for four, I will not reverse my decree;[a] because they have threshed Gilead[b] with threshing-sledges of iron. So I will send 4 a fire upon the house of Hazael, and it shall devour the strong-holds of Ben-hadad. I will break the bar of Damascus, and cut 5 off him that sits on the throne[c] from Biq'ath-awen and him that holds the sceptre from Beth-eden; and the people of Syria shall go into exile to Kir', says the LORD.

Against the Philistines

Thus says the LORD: 'For three transgressions of Gaza and for 1.6 four, I will not reverse my decree; because they carried into exile a whole people to deliver them up to Edom. So I will 7 send a fire upon the wall of Gaza, which will devour her strong-holds. I will cut off him that sits on the throne from Ashod, 8 and him that holds the sceptre from Ashkelon; I will turn my hand against Ekron; and the remnant of the Philistines shall perish', says the LORD.[d]

Against Tyre

Thus says the LORD: 'For three transgressions of Tyre and for 1.9 four, I will not reverse my decree; because they delivered up a whole people to Edom,[e] and did not remember the covenant

16

of brotherhood. I will send a fire upon the walls of Tyre, and   10
it shall devour her strongholds.'

Against Edom

Thus says the LORD: 'For three transgressions of Edom and for   1.11
four, I will not reverse my decree; because he pursued his
brother with the sword, and cast away his obligations towards
him, and his anger tore perpetually, and he kept his wrath for
ever. So I will send a fire upon Teman, and it shall devour the   12
strongholds of Bozrah.'

Against the Ammonites

Thus says the LORD: 'For three transgressions of the Ammo-   1.13
nites and for four, I will not reverse my decree; because they
have ripped up women with child in Gilead that they might
enlarge their border. So I will kindle a fire in the wall of   14
Rabbah, and it shall devour her strongholds, with shouting
in the day of battle, with a tempest in the day of the whirl-
wind; their king shall go into exile, he and his princes
together', says the LORD.

Against the Moabites

Thus says the LORD: 'For three transgressions of Moab and for   2.1
four, I will not reverse my decree; because he burnt to lime
the bones of the king of Edom. So I will send a fire upon   2
Moab, and it shall devour the strongholds of Kerioth, and
Moab shall die amid uproar, amid shouting and the sound of
the trumpet; I will cut off the ruler from its midst, and slay   3
all its princes with him', says the LORD.

Against Judah

Thus says the LORD: 'For three transgressions of Judah and   2.4
for four, I will not reverse my decree; because they have
rejected the law of the LORD, and have not kept his statutes,
but their idols have led them astray, after which their fathers
walked. But I will send fire upon Judah, and it shall devour   5
the strongholds of Jerusalem.'

Notes on the translation

a. The highly elliptical phrase לא אשיבנו presents some problems of exegesis. We cannot do better than follow Wolff's account of the various interpretations it has received:

(i) 'I will not make the Assyrians return from attacking them' - thus H. W. Hogg.[1] This has little plausibility.

(ii) 'I will not let the deported population of Damascus return' - thus the Jewish commentators, Rashi, Ibn Ezra, Kimhi. This will work in the first oracle, but cannot be made to apply in the oracles where there is no mention of exile.

(iii) 'I will not return a favourable answer' - this is the view of Néher,[2] who sees Amos as a cult prophet whom the nations come to consult for an oracle from Yahweh. This stands or falls with the whole question of the plausibility of seeing Amos as a cult prophet, which we have already discussed.

(iv) 'I will not make them return to me' - thus Morgenstern.[3] This is clearly a possible sense, but (i) the meaning of the oracle is obscured: while this phrase speaks of Yahweh's abandoning the nations to their sin, in the sequel he intervenes to punish by fire, and (ii) the nations are generally spoken of either in the plural (על־דושם) or in the feminine singular (על־ארמנותיה), rarely in the masculine singular (1.11, 2.1).

(v) 'I will not withdraw the punishment' - thus RV, NEB ('I will grant them no reprieve'), and many commentators from Wellhausen to Cripps. There is a good deal to be said in favour of this exegesis. Whether the punishment is seen as following inexorably on the crime, or as imposed by Yahweh, or both, does not matter: Yahweh refuses to 'recall' it. This is the most obvious sense of the passage, unless it is given a little more accurately by

(vi) 'I will not rescind my decree' - thus Wolff, Weiser,[4] and the wordy Jerusalem Bible rendering 'I have made my decree and will not relent.' 7.2f and 5f, and 8.2, suggest that Amos had once seen some possibility of Yahweh's altering his decision to punish Israel, but had become convinced that the time for such change of heart was past. Similarly here with the nations: Yahweh has decreed their destruction, and will not alter his decree. Compare Numbers 23.20b, in the Balaam oracles, where לא אשיבנה is connected with 19a 'God . . . will not repent (נחם).'

b. The Septuagint has τὰς ἐν γαστρὶ ἐχούσας ἐν Γαλααδ, but compare 1.13, though K. Budde[5] defends the LXX against MT.

c. The singular יושב in parallel with תומך־שבט suggests this sense, against Septuagint τοὺς κατοικοῦντας (thus Wolff in his commentary, compare RV Margin and JB).

d. Omitting אדני with the LXX.

e. אדום is again sometimes emended to ארם on grounds of geographical probability (Maag[6] and Robinson[7]); the false pointing is explained as due to influence from 1.6. This makes good sense but must remain doubtful; in any case much depends on the dating and authenticity of the oracle.[8]

f. שְׁמָרָה is odd. Wolff suggests pointing שָׁמְרָה, 'his anger kept watch', i.e. 'did not rest'; but most commentators follow Olshausen in reading שָׁמַר לָנֶצַח (compare BHS).

Exegesis

Aram

The crime of 'threshing' Gilead is variously taken as a metaphor for harsh treatment in war (Nowack,[9] Weiser[10]), or as a literal description of torture meted out to prisoners of war (thus the Targum, which reads 'the inhabitants of Gilead'); Harper[11] gives details of the kinds of threshing instrument which might have been used to inflict it. Edghill[12] and Wolff suggest it is a metaphor, which nonetheless corresponds pretty closely to the kind of treatment captives could expect. Tiglath-pileser I once uses the same imagery: 'the land Bit-Amukkani I threshed as with a threshing instrument; all its people and its possessions I brought to Assyria';[13] compare also in a vassal treaty of Esarhaddon: 'May Shamash with an iron plough (cut up) your cities (and your districts)'.[14] But the explicit 'threshing sledges of iron' seems to suggest a quite literal interpretation.

Biq'ath-awen and Beth-eden present difficulties. It has been common to identify the latter as the Aramaean state of Bit-Adini, which since 856 B.C. had been an Assyrian province ruled latterly by the brilliant governor Shamshi-ilu (773–746).[15] This identification is generally accepted at II Kings 19.12 and Ezekiel 27.23, and is supported in this verse by Wolff. The LXX (ἐξ ἀνδρῶν χαρραν) evidently thought the same. But this interpretation has been challenged by M. Haran,[16] who points out that the comparatively distant Bit-Adini could be implicated in the crimes of Aram-Damascus only if Amos were lumping all the Aramaeans together indiscriminately; which would be specially inept in view of Bit-Adini's status as an Assyrian province, having nothing to do with the king in Damascus or with the line of Hazael and Ben-hadad. No one 'held the sceptre' in Til-Barsip. Gottwald's proposal[17] that Bit-Adini may have been allied with Damascus in Amos's day would seem to be impossible. Haran considers rather that we should see the names as deliberate corruptions by the prophet of hated features of Aram-Damascus. אָוֶן is used for just such a purpose in Hosea 4.15 (Beth-aven for Bethel), and the reference here is probably to the plain between Lebanon and Anti-Lebanon (el-beqa', the בקעת־הלבנון of Joshua 11.17). In that the case the Vulgate may be right in rendering בית־עדן as *de domo voluptatis* (pointing עֵדֶן), possibly a derisive reference to the royal palace. Certainly this gives a much more limited denunciation of Aram-Damascus, rather than of the entire Aramaean area, and I think is to be preferred. Of course none of this argument will hold if the prophet is here taking over an older oracle.

Philistia

There is some doubt about the exact nature of the crime here referred to. The root סגר in Deuteronomy 23.15 and Obadiah 14 means 'hand over (a fugitive to his rightful sovereign)', and the Aramaic cognate סכר is so used in the Sefire treaties to refer to extradition.[18] Néher supposes the verb to bear the same sense here. But it is difficult to see how any sense can be made of the oracle on this interpretation of it; it must surely be meant to refer to the common practice of turning captured enemies into slaves.[19] There is no indication in the text which nation was handed over to the Edomites; and, as so often in the Old Testament, it has sometimes been conjectured that we should read 'Aram' for 'Edom': on both these points, see below, p. 31.

Tyre

Again there is no way of telling what גלות שלמה refers to: certainly it does not demonstrably mean that Tyre sold Israelites to Edom. Nowack and Edghill pointed out that it could well refer to oppression by Tyre of other Phoenician cities; in the seventh century Tyre assisted Assyria in suppressing rebellion in the surrounding country, and her own destruction was due to a largely Phoenician army. Such interpretations explain the phrase ברית־אחים as a reference to the racial ties between Tyre and those she oppressed. On the other hand more recent studies have made it clear that אָח can be a technical term for 'treaty partner', regardless of actual blood relationship: compare I Kings 20.32 and ANET 199f, 201f (the treaty between Rameses II and Hattusilis III) and the extensive evidence cited by Fishbane.[20] This makes it clear that Nowack's explanation, though attractive, is not necessitated by the text, whose exact reference remains obscure. Tyre has broken a treaty with another state by selling its inhabitants to Edom (or possibly Aram); which state, we do not know.[21]

Edom

The sense of וְשִׁחֵת רַחֲמָיו is obscure: the Septuagint renders καὶ
ἐλυμήνατο μήτραν ἐπὶ γῆς (compare Vulgate), construing רחמיו directly
from רֶחֶם ; Pesiqta Rabbati 48a says that Esau ripped his mother's womb
when he was born, indicating a similar exegesis. The easiest interpretation
is from רחמים ; thus NEB 'stifling their natural affections'. Fishbane
cites frequent uses of *ra'amu* in treaty contexts: thus in the Amarna Letters the combination *ra'á'-mu-ta ù ahu-ut-ta*, 'friendship and brotherhood',
is frequent; and compare Elephantine Papyrus 408, where רחמן can be
construed as 'treaty recognition'.[22] Probably, therefore, as in the preceding oracle the breaking of a treaty is meant, and this is confirmed by the
use of אָח (see above). Once again it is not quite certain who Edom's
'brother' is meant to be, but the frequent occurrence of the theme of
Israel's brotherhood with Edom in the Old Testament suggests that, quite
apart from the treaty background, it is Israel that is intended.

Ammon

This oracle requires little comment here. The crime denounced is mentioned a number of times in the Old Testament – e.g. II Kings 15.16,[23]
and see below, p. 57.

Moab

Weiser says that the bones were soaked in lime to burn them: the Targum
makes the gruesome suggestion that they were used for making lime to
whitewash the Moabite king's house. Generally commentators take לשיד
as an indication of the complete destruction of the bones – compare
Vulgate *usque ad cinerem*. In any case the crime consisted of defiling the
corpse, whether this is felt as wicked because of the disrespect it implies
towards a fallen enemy, or because of the idea that the unburied dead do
not rest. This cannot be regarded as in any sense a crime against Israel;
Würthwein's suggestion[24] that Edom's special relationship with Israel
('brotherhood') makes any crime against her automatically a crime against
Israel rests rather on his theory of a cultic provenance for the oracles
against the nations than on any indications in the text. It is of course
possible that the Massoretic pointing here represents a misunderstanding of
an original *molk 'dm*; this is suggested by Torczyner.[25] The reference might
then be, as suggested by J. R. Bartlett,[26] to the action of Mesha, II Kings
3.27, but this is by no means certain: see below, pp. 33–5.

Judah

This oracle presents no textual or exegetical problems; but as we shall argue there is a very high likelihood that it is not authentic.

Authenticity

It is extremely hard to establish any objective criteria for deciding on the authenticity of particular prophetic oracles. Nevertheless it may be worth trying to distinguish between arguments based on syntactic and poetic structure and historical content, on the one hand, and those which avowedly rest on some particular theory of construction and *Sitz im Leben,* on the other. On purely historical grounds only one oracle is really suspect, that against Edom. Its most obvious setting is in the exilic situation, and on these grounds Nowack, Marti,[27] Fosbroke,[28] Weiser, Wolff, and Mays[29] all argue that it is not by Amos. As we shall see, there is a possibility that the aggression by Edom is to be located in the rebellion mentioned in II Kings 8.20, or that it does not refer to hostility against Israel at all but against some other ally of Edom; but on the whole the argument for an exilic date has much to commend it. In any case literary arguments can be brought to tip the scales. No doubt Amos may have varied his style of address, but still the impression left by this oracle and the preceding one, against Tyre, is distinctly different from that made by other oracles in 1.2–2.3. Wolff[30] notes three differences in the Tyre and Edom oracles, viz.:

(a) the infinitive clause with על- is expanded with one or more finite verbs:

(b) the threat of punishment is shorter: it repeats only the elements common to all the oracles, and does not particularise;

(c) the final אמר יהוה is missing.

In addition the crime in the Tyre oracle is the same as that in the preceding one on Philistia; and though for lack of evidence we may not accept Wolff's suggestion that הגלה גלות is avoided because, in the exilic period, it had become a technical term for exile to Babylon, so that the Philistines could only 'deliver up' fugitives from the greater deportation, yet הסגירם גלות שלמה does read awkwardly, and gives rise to the suspicion that it is an abbreviation of the charge in the preceding oracles. A further small point made by Wolff is worth noting: the phrase זכר ברית is not otherwise attested before the priestly writer (e.g. Genesis 9.15f; Exodus 2.24; Leviticus 26.42).

Commentators are by no means agreed in deleting these oracles,[31] though the trend seems to be in that direction. On the whole we may decide to agree with Weiser and Wolff and deny them to Amos on literary and historical grounds.

The Judah oracle is much more generally dismissed as inauthentic, whether for its style, strongly reminiscent of the Deuteronomic historian, or for its insipid content (I am inclined to think the latter is the more convincing argument). It is hard to believe that Amos could not have found some more definite sin with which to charge Judah, and in any case the tone of general disapprobation for disobedience to law is quite out of keeping with the indictment of the other nations for war crimes (foreign nations) and social injustice (Israel).[32] In addition much the same literary considerations apply here as for the Tyre and Edom oracles.

The only other of the oracles whose authenticity has been seriously questioned is 1.6-8, against the Philistines. Here the argument is a mixture of literary/historical considerations and rather more tendentious theory. Marti,[33] following Duhm,[34] argued that the historical circumstances are not those of Amos's day, since Gath is not mentioned. It was not destroyed until 711 (by Sargon) and the oracle must consequently be later than this. Furthermore, the verses composing the Philistine oracle 'lack the originality of the prophet Amos';[35] they are based on Joel 3.4-8. But the most important factor is the geographical progression of the oracles, and the structure of the whole passage. If the oracles on Philistia, Tyre and Edom are omitted, the cycle follows a natural geographical progression - Aram, Ammon, Moab, Israel; and the three ten-line strophes of the Israel oracle are paralleled by three ten-line strophes on the nations.

It is doubtful whether anyone now pays any attention to Marti's hypotheses, since such wholesale deletion of prophetic oracles on *a priori* grounds went out of favour. Its strongest point is the absence of Gath, but there might be any number of reasons for Amos to pass it over in silence. Amos himself, in 6.2, suggests that Gath had already been damaged enough to serve as a typical example of helplessness. This could refer to its capture by Uzziah, reported in II Chronicles 26.6. Marti further argues that it is reasonable for an Old Testament writer to worry about geographical progression, and we may agree that there can be no grounds for denying the possibility; only we should look to see if he has in fact done so. Similarly Marti's strophic arrangement is very effective and satisfying; but there is no reason to think that it was also Amos's.

But the geographical hypothesis needs to be mentioned if only because it is a two-edged sword; for in Bentzen's hands it became the means of defending the authenticity of the whole section.[36] We have already suggested that Bentzen's arguments are far from compelling and that the order in which the nations are named is probably more or less arbitrary, or that other considerations than geography have been taken into account. Both edges of this particular sword are blunt, and we make no progress by using it.

So we conclude that the Judah oracle is certainly, the Edom oracle almost certainly, and the Tyre oracle very probably, not by Amos; the other oracles are authentic words of the prophet.

CHAPTER 4

In discussing possible derivations for these oracles against the nations, we argued that they are not in any simple sense directed against 'Israel's enemies'; all the nations named had indeed been at war with Israel at some time but they were not all currently opposing Israel by force. At best we could speak of 'Israel's traditional enemies'. On the other hand it is clear that all the nations in question had at some time perpetrated atrocities, whether against Israel or against their other neighbours, which Amos could count on his hearers' being familiar with and scandalised at. We now have to ask, when did these atrocities take place, and in what context?[1]

The traditional view has been that Amos is here referring to events from the far distant past, probably from the previous century, and that the period of the 'Aramaean wars', in the regions of Ahab, Ahaziah, Joram, and Jehu of Israel, especially the latter part of this period (say the 850s onwards), would fit best.[2] Clements argues for a still earlier date: 'Some obscurity regarding the precise historical context of these crimes remains, but the indications are that they had all taken place long before the time of Amos, probably more than a century before . . . they represented traditional examples of inhuman conduct.'[3] By 'more than a century' Clements implies that they took place during the break-up of the Solomonic empire in the early ninth century.[4] Wolff, however, has argued that it is more likely that Amos would appeal to contemporary or near-contemporary events, and that a place can be found for most of these atrocities during the reign of Jeroboam II.[5]

It is probably unwise to argue this case on *a priori* grounds. In any case we have no way of knowing that all the events referred to took place in the same period; they could, for example, be the most recent memorable atrocity in each case. It will be better, therefore, to examine each oracle in its own right. We will not attempt a general sketch of the period: Wolff provides an excellent one, and for the most recent detailed survey see Herrmann's *History of Israel.*[6] As Herrmann himself points out, however, the period from the revolt of Jehu to the accession of Jeroboam II is unfortunately a very obscure one, and it will be surprising if we can come to any firm conclusions.

On Aram

The Aramaeans are accused of 'threshing Gilead'. The Aramaean wars with the Israelite kings present great problems to the historian, partly because the Old Testament accounts of them seem to have suffered dislocation through the editors' desire to associate them with events in the careers of Elijah and Elisha, partly because the memory of numerous similar campaigns seems to have become vague and muddled. 'We gain the impression that a variety of reminiscences were current of the considerable political activities of the Aramaeans of Damascus and the battles which extended all over Transjordania, in which troops from both Israel and Judah were involved.'[8] Nevertheless Old Testament scholars have generally thought of three main periods of Aramaean expansion, in which attacks on Gilead to the south would have been likely.

(1) The first has its roots as far back as the reign of Solomon, and was in part responsible for the break-up of the Davidic–Solomonic empire. This is Clements's 'more than a century before' Amos. According to I Kings 11.23-6 Solomon had to face attack from Rezon ben Eliada, who seceded from Aram-Zobah and asserted his rule over the kingdom of Aram-Damascus;[9] possibly Solomon lost most of eastern Syria.[10] By the reigns of Asa and Baasha the Aramaeans were sufficiently strong to intervene on behalf of Judah in a border dispute (I Kings 15.18-22). The Old Testament does not mention any attacks on Gileadite territory in this period, but the possibility cannot be dismissed out of hand.

(2) The second period is during the reign of Ahab, when according to I Kings 20 and 22 Israel fought the Aramaeans at Aphek, east of Lake Gennesaret, and at Ramoth-gilead. Here one has the impression that both sides are over-stretched and prepared to make concessions, provided that prestige is not lost; but the truces are uneasy (I Kings 20.34). Aramaean expansion is curtailed by the threat of the rising Assyrian power under Shalmaneser III, which makes itself felt in Palestinian affairs for the first time at the battle of Qarqar (853) at the end of Ahab's reign, linking Aram and Israel in an *ad hoc* coalition.[11] This coalition lasted until at least 845.[12] Recent studies have made it doubtful whether this period can be considered very seriously as the background to Amos's oracles, since it is not clear that the Old Testament is right to attribute Transjordanian campaigns to the reign of Ahab at all. J. M. Miller,[13] noticing the vagueness of attribution to 'the king of Israel' in I Kings 20 and 22, argues that these chapters preserve all that was remembered of the three victories against

the Aramaeans predicted by Elisha in II Kings 13.19, which occurred in the reigns of either Jehoahaz or Jehoash. The misplacing is readily explicable on the hypothesis of a southern collector for these traditions who did not know which 'king of Israel' was intended, but who noted that he was allied to 'the king of Judah' and too hastily assumed that this latter must be Jehoshaphat (cf. I Kings 22.2–4; the same applies to the Moabite campaign of II Kings 3). The difficulties which this theory removes are many. There is no longer any need to postulate a multiplicity of Ben-hadads; nor is any complicated explanation needed why Ahab's Aramaean opponent is called Ben-hadad in I Kings while his ally at Qarqar, who must be the same man, is called by the Assyrians Adad-idri (= Hebrew Hadadezer).[14] Instead we have a simple succession: Hadadezer, Hazael, Ben-hadad.[15] Furthermore, the Israelite–Aramaean alliance need no longer be regarded as an *ad hoc* affair, but as a settled policy, and this also fits in much better with the Assyrian evidence that Qarqar was not Shalmaneser III's only encounter with this confederacy of Syrian and Palestinian kingdoms[16] – that it formed in fact a recognisable political entity. As to the general likelihood of Transjordanian campaigns under Ahab, it may be noted that II Kings 10.32–3 seems to imply that the whole of Gilead was safely in Israelite hands until the rise of Hazael; and I Kings 21.27–9 may be taken as indicating that the Deuteronomic historian supposed Ahab to have died in his bed – the story of his repentance being recorded precisely to explain this surprising fact.[17] Of course we cannot say with certainty that Ahab did not fight the Aramaeans, but the difficulties in supposing him to have done so are very considerable.

(3) The third period of Aramaean expansion began with the accession of the usurper Hazael,[18] who abandoned the alliance with Israel and once more launched an attack on Gilead (II Kings 8.28f). After reverses against the Assyrians in 841 and 838 he again attacked Transjordania (II Kings 10.32f) and even invaded Israel up to the borders of Judah (II Kings 12.17f). This period of Aramaean ascendancy is said to have lasted through the reigns of Joram, Jehu and Jehoahaz, ending around 802 with the conquests of Adad-nirari III.[19] It is to this period that most scholars attribute the atrocity against Gilead in Amos 1.3.

In fact the picture is again complicated. At the very beginning of this period we have II Kings 8.28, which records how Ahab's son Joram formed an alliance with Ahaziah ben Jehoram of Judah to fight Hazael, and the immediate sequel to this is the rise of Jehu, so that it must be dated 843/2, presumably during a lull in Shalmaneser's campaigns and not long before his victory recorded on the Black Obelisk. Miller thinks that this battle at Ramoth-gilead is one of the two conflated in I Kings 22. It is in

Jehu's reign that Transjordania was gradually lost to Israel, according to II Kings 10.32-3; but Herrmann points out that there are no actual accounts of Aramaean attacks on Israelite towns from this period,[20] and it may be that a considerable break in hostilities followed the isolated campaign of Joram. It is a question just how long Aramaean domination lasted in the area. II Kings 13.5 may be taken as an indication that Jehoahaz himself began to throw off the Aramaean yoke, whereas according to 13.19 and 13.25 it was his son Jehoash who first began to beat them in battle. Miller argues that the first suggestion is the correct one, and that it was in fact Jehoahaz who won the three victories predicted by Elisha, the prophet dying during his reign, somewhere before 799/8. I doubt if the text is in fact so contradictory as he supposes. In view of II Kings 13.7, it seems rather unlikely that Jehoahaz should have been able to *defeat* the Aramaeans; and 13.4-5 suggests not that he regained any lost possession, say in Transjordania, but only that under him Israel 'escaped from the hand of the Aramaeans'. This is perhaps most readily understood as meaning that Aramaean armies ceased actually to *invade* Israel, and it would still be reasonable to associate the recovery of Israelite independence with the reign of Jehoash.[21] It is possible that we have more information about Israel's 'deliverance' under Jehoahaz in a garbled form elsewhere in Kings. Miller himself argues, as we have seen, that I Kings 20.1-21 ought to be placed in the reign of Jehoahaz (Ben-hadad having succeeded Hazael during Jehu's reign). A siege of Samaria by the Aramaeans is quite conceivable in this time of Israelite weakness: note the smallness of 'Ahab's' army in 20.27 (cf. II Kings 13.7). According to II Kings 12.17 Aramaean troops overran Palestine as far as Gaza, and took tribute from Jehoahaz's contemporary Joash of Judah.

But a further complication is surely introduced by the narrative of II Kings 6.24-7.20.[22] This looks very like another version of the siege in I Kings 20.1-21, slanted towards Elisha and attributing the deliverance to a 'rumour' in the manner of II Kings 19.7. If this is in fact a variant version of Jehoahaz's deliverance from Aram we should probably conclude with Miller that Elisha is the 'saviour' of II Kings 13.5; but there is little difficulty in thinking that the rumour of attack by 'kings of Hatti and Musri' is a garbled reference to Adad-nirari's attack on Damascus. I Kings 20 continues in vv. 22-43 with a battle of Israel against Aram at Aphek in northern Transjordania, which puts a decisive end to the period of Aramaean oppression, and opens up the way for a subsequent battle at Ramoth-gilead (I Kings 22). Aphek can easily be attributed either to Jehoahaz or to Jehoash (see below). I Kings 22 presents more problems.

Miller argues that it conflates two battles in Gilead: first, the battle in which Joram of Israel and Ahaziah of Judah joined forces (see above) – and this battle results in defeat; second, a battle led by Jehoahaz with help from Joash. We can no longer tell what was the outcome of this battle, but it seems more than likely (against Miller) that it too resulted in defeat for Israel. Miller points out that the prophet Micaiah is placed in the custody of 'Amon, the governor of the city, and Joash, the king's son' (I Kings 22.26), and argues that this Joash may well be the J(eh)oash who succeeded Jehoahaz – no recondite exegesis of בֶּן־הַמֶּלֶךְ is needed.[23] But if this is so, Micaiah's gloomy prophecy must be associated with the Jehoahaz–Joash alliance rather than with Joram–Ahaziah: and it is reasonable to think that the story was recorded because the prophecy was fulfilled, and Israel routed. Plainly there is now small chance of untangling this chapter, but it does seem unlikely that it contains a record of an Israelite *victory* at Ramoth-gilead. It looks as though Jehoahaz's victory at Aphek, if such there was, was only a temporary *setback* for Ben-hadad, as the prophet of I Kings 20.42 seems to suggest. Indeed it would be simpler to attribute it to Jehoash; there is no insuperable objection to this on literary grounds, since the link in I Kings 20 between vv.1–21 and vv.22–43 is clearly loose. We might then be able to trace an abortive campaign against the Aramaeans in Gilead; a subsequent weakening of Aramaean power in the last days of Jehoahaz's reign, with the siege of Samaria thwarted by domestic trouble, probably the attack of Adad-nirari; and a qualified victory for Jehoash at Aphek about the turn of the century, recovering Israel's independence as predicted by Elisha in II Kings 13.17. This, I think, is as coherent as Miller's hypothesis, and does not entail any re-arrangement of II Kings 13. Jehoash then followed up his victory at Aphek with two other campaigns and recovered 'the cities which (Ben-hadad) had taken from his father Jehoahaz in war' – possibly including some in Transjordania, if it was indeed under Jehoahaz that these had been lost.

The effect of the reconstruction so far has been to bring the whole of the Aramaean wars down to a later period than has usually been assigned to them, beginning perhaps not until quite late in Jehu's reign (with the exception of Jehoram's battle at Ramoth-gilead) and reaching their height under Jehoahaz and Jehoash. There is no doubt that there is plenty of scope for placing Amos's reference to an Aramaean invasion of Gilead in the days of Jehoahaz. However, a third possibility has since been suggested and is developed by M. Haran:[24] he suggests that it was only under Jeroboam II that Israel began to regain its holdings in Transjordania; for it was he who according to II Kings 14.25 'restored the border of Israel from Lebo-hamath[25] as far as the Sea of Arabah'. The burden of Haran's argument is that the 'Indian summer' theory of Jeroboam's reign is not tenable in the light of Assyrian expansion during this period, and that it was not until almost the end of his life that Jeroboam was in fact free to pursue his plans for expansion. He suggests that some attacks on Transjordania may have been possible during the reign of Assur-dan III (771/2-754/5), though even he invaded Syria, but that no real Israelite conquest of Damascus and Hamath can be envisaged before the time of his successor Assur-nirari V (753/4-745/6), who left Syria–Palestine entirely unmolested for a brief period before Tiglath-pileser III succeeded him. This would mean that Jeroboam's celebrated 'empire' lasted no more than seven or eight years; it would also mean that the Aramaeans could have retained control or at least freedom of movement – hence freedom to plunder and pillage – in Gilead and the rest of Transjordania until as late as the 750s.

It is not clear, however, that even Haran's estimate of the political situation in the first half of the eighth century does justice to its complexities, for there is the additional factor of Urartu to be reckoned with. The partial recovery of Israel's fortunes under Jehoash is indeed readily explained by the ascendancy of Adad-nirari III and his stranglehold on the Aramaean states; and similarly for later achievements, such as the recovery of Transjordanian territory, a powerful Assyria would have been a help rather than a hindrance to Israel. It was in periods of Assyrian quiescence that the Aramaeans were able to assert their power by striking south into Gilead, in periods of Assyrian ascendancy that Israel might strike back and expect to win. Assyrian control over Aram-Damascus lasted until Adad-nirari's death in 782, but by 773 Urartu under Sardur III seems to have reduced Assyria under Shalmaneser IV to a position where it is possible that the Aramaeans were able to attack her themselves.[26] As Haran rightly observes, the ensuing period under Assur-dan III and Assur-nirari V was not one during which Jeroboam is likely to have made much headway in Transjordania, but this is because Aramaean power was then once again unleashed, rather than because the Assyrians themselves posed any threat as he seems to suggest.[27] From 773 until the rise of Tiglath-pileser III Aram was once more free to involve itself in affairs east of the Jordan, and Israel could not count on any stronger power to bind it. If Jeroboam did 'capture' Damascus, as II Kings 14.28 claims, Israel had lost all hold on it again by the time Tiglath-pileser came to conquer it: and it seems probable that the biblical account of his empire is somewhat exaggerated. The truth would rather seem to be that neither Israel nor Aram held the ascendancy in these years of Assyrian decline under the shadow of Urartu, but that there was sporadic fighting between them: so that we should reckon with a second period of Aramaean aggression, separated by only a few years from the end of the first in the days of Jehoash.

The advantage of this scheme from the point of view of interpreting Amos is clear. In 6.13–14 he refers to Israelite victories in Transjordania which must be recent if his comments are to have any point: the people pride themselves on the conquest of Lo-debar and Qarnaim,[28] cities apparently reclaimed from the Aramaeans during Jeroboam's attempts to secure the other side of the Jordan. It would be quite in keeping with this if he were countering Aramaean aggression in the same area, repelling an Aramaean advance into Gilead. Of recent commentators, Wolff favours this dating for the events referred to in Amos 1.3, and there is no difficulty about accepting it as a possibility.[29]

We may conclude, then, that Amos 1.3 may refer either to nearly contemporary events or to Aramaean expansion in the days of Jehu or Jehoahaz some forty to fifty years earlier, or possibly to much earlier events in the break-up of Solomon's empire. We must now examine the other historical allusions, and for this the historical outline as so far drawn will prove useful.

On Philistia

Our information about Aram-Damascus in the ninth to eighth centuries is copious but confused; but when we turn to the other nations condemned by Amos, evidence is simply very scanty. The Philistines are accused, apparently, of handing over prisoners of war either to Edom or to Aram.[30] Of contacts between Philistines and Edom we know nothing. If the reading 'Aram' is preferred, there is a possible occasion for such trading during the reign of Hazael. According to II Kings 12.17–18, as we have seen, Hazael went on raids as far as Gath during the reign of Joash of Judah, and was only prevented from attacking Jerusalem too when Joash bought him off; this extension of Aramaean power fits in well with what we can reconstruct of the reigns of Jehoahaz and Joash from elsewhere. It is possible that the Philistines paid Hazael a tribute of slaves at this time. Nothing in the texts suggests that these slaves were Israelite or Judaean prisoners, but if they were they could possibly have been captured at the time of Philistine raids on Judah during Jehoram's reign, reported in II Chronicles 21.16–17, some time during the 840s, or in subsequent raids unknown to us. If, however, the reference is to friendly trade[31] between the Philistines and Aram, we can do nothing to date it.

On Tyre

The historical reference in this oracle, which we have judged probably inauthentic, is totally obscure. Most oracles against Tyre seem to post-date the accession of Nebuchadnezzar II (604) – see Wolff, *ad loc.*

On Edom

Again we have presented literary reasons for thinking this oracle secon-dary, and if these are accepted then it will probably fall into the large cate-gory of anti-Edomite oracles composed during the exilic age and reflecting that Edomite involvement in the sack of Jerusalem recorded in Obadiah 11. However, if the literary problems are ignored, a case can be made out for an earlier reference. Kaufmann[32] suggests that Edom's breach with Judah in the reign of Jehoram (II Kings 8.20) is in Amos's mind here, in which case the date might be close to that of the Philistine atrocity. Haran thinks rather in terms of Amaziah's Edomite war (II Kings 14.7; cf. II Chronicles 25.11–12) and of atrocities evidently committed by Edomites while engaged in it. This seems a little unlikely, since the Old Testament accounts consistently present it as a war of aggression by Judah. Memories of numerous unrecorded border raids could be at the back of this oracle, and in that case no specific period can be suggested: but I still prefer to explain the oracle as exilic.

On Ammon

Here we are back with material whose authenticity there is no reason to dispute. But once again the incident referred to, apparently so specific, has as its background the never-ending border disputes between Gilead and Ammon. The most that can be said is that Ammonite incursions into Gilead are most likely to have occurred in periods when Transjordania was not engaging the attention of empire-builders: and this might be thought to tend against a dating in the days of Hazael, as argued by Gottwald. Hazael himself practised this particular atrocity (compare II Kings 8.12), and so did the Israelite king Menahem in Isaiah's day (II Kings 15.16); and Gottwald makes the interesting suggestion that warfare in Transjordan tended to run more readily to such brutality, and that its inhabitants were regarded by the more sophisticated states in Palestine and Syria as mere barbarians. As we saw above, the period immediately before Amos, when Urartu held Assyria in check and freed the Aramaeans once more, was pro-bably a time when many petty states could harass unprotected areas across the Jordan, and so we might well follow Wolff in placing this atrocity here. But again, many datings are possible.

On Moab

If מלך־אדם is understood as 'a human sacrifice', then there is no certain way of dating the reference. It might be a quite general criticism of Moabite religious practice, though the other crimes mentioned in these oracles are apparently more specific, and all concerned with international relations. The only recorded instance of such a sacrifice is in II Kings 3.27, during the Moabite campaign of the Israel–Judah–Edom coalition. Since this or its aftermath has also been suggested as the context for the 'burning of the king of Edom's bones' which, following MT, is more commonly thought to be the crime condemned here, we must look at it in more detail. Taking II Kings 3 as it stands it is Mesha, the only Moabite king whose name is recorded in the Old Testament, that sacrificed his son in order to turn back the coalition's advance; but as with the accounts of the Omride period already discussed, there is some reason to suspect that the narrative was originally anonymous.[33] Five arguments are set out by K.-H. Bernhardt[34] to suggest a later date than the reigns of Jehoshaphat and Mesha:

(i) It is very unlikely that the coalition would have attacked Moab from the south had any other route been open to them, for the chances of a successful onslaught *via* the steep ascent of the rift of the Arabah was very slight, and (as 3.21 confirms) surprise was impossible. This suggests a time when the routes into Moab from the north were held by some foreign power, i.e. after the gradual loss of Transjordanian holdings in the reign of Jehu at the earliest.[35]

(ii) Since an attack from the south entailed a much heavier burden and greater danger for Judah than for Israel, the king of Judah must either have been a vassal of Israel or have had a paramount interest himself in keeping the Moabites under control. Neither of these alternatives is readily compatible with the confident reign of Jehoshaphat; Judaean internal weakness, combined with such a loss of control on Transjordania as to involve the risk of border raids, is much more easily fitted into the reign of Joash (836/5-797/6) – compare II Kings 12.17 – or of his son Amaziah.

(iii) According to I Kings 22.47f Jehoshaphat had turned Edom into a province under a Judaean governor, so that there will have been no 'king of Edom' until the Edomite rebellion under his son Jehoram (850/49-843/2). This does not of itself necessitate a very much later date than the narrator suggests, but it does tend to favour the original anonymity of the king of Judah in the account, and hence to open the door for different datings. Furthermore the king of Edom must have felt threatened as seriously as the king of Judah, which supports point (ii).

(iv) Judah and Edom can hardly have wished to capture Moab in order to subjugate it to Israel; everything in the narrative, especially the desperate character of the campaign, suggests that self-defence rather than expansion was the motive; and the scorched-earth policy advocated by Elisha (II Kings 3.18–19) supports the view that the object is the annihilation rather than the annexation of Moab.[36] This again tends to argue for a date later than the reigns of Jehoshaphat and Joram. II Kings 13.20f reports that Moabite bands were invading Israelite territory in the period when Elisha *died*. Even if we take the view that Elisha was buried in Gilead,[37] this would suggest that they were a severe hazard; while on Bernhardt's own suggestion that Elisha was buried at Jericho, the place where his master Elijah had left him (cf. II Kings 2), they would clearly have been dangerous enough to warrant an expedition even as hazardous as that of II Kings 3. We may be able to gain further support from II Chronicles 20, where Judah, too, under Jehoshaphat has to face attacks from Moabites and Ammonites. It is noteworthy that the campaign of II Kings 3 is absent from the Chronicler's work, and it is tempting to see this narrative as a substitute for it, which has the advantage of omitting any suggestion of an alliance between the pious Jehoshaphat and the apostate northern kingdom. II Chronicles 20.10 and 22 maintain that the 'men of Mount Seir' joined the Moabite-Ammonite coalition against Judah, but in v.23 the coalition falls apart and the 'men of Mount Seir' are destroyed by their allies. It is not far-fetched to think that the Chronicler might thus have scrambled II Kings 3, veiling the true reason for Moabite destruction of Edom, her alliance with Judah, which again would have reflected on Jehoshaphat's religious purity.[38] This campaign could well be the one in which Moabites burned the king of Edom's bones, as suggested above. The whole complex of II Kings 3 and II Chronicles 20 would therefore fit well into the period around the death of Elisha, which could have been as late as the beginning of the reign of Jehoash (799/8–784/3), if the foregoing reconstruction of the Aramaean wars is accepted.

(v) Finally, Bernhardt argues that Joram could not have attacked Moab since throughout his reign he was fully engaged either in

fighting in the Aramaean coalition against the Assyrians, like
father Ahab, or in rebelling against Aram and trying to recapture
territory in Gilead (II Kings 8.28f and 9.14). This does not seem
fully convincing, since the Gileadite campaign of II Kings 8.28f is
clearly Joram's last, and there might be a gap of a year or two
between his leaving the Aramaean coalition and his attempt to
regain Ramoth-gilead, a gap into which the Moabite campaign
could be fitted. But Bernhardt clearly has a point. The reigns of
Jehu and Jehoahaz see both Hebrew kingdoms too weak for such
an undertaking; it is only after the victories over Aram, which we
have suggested were won by Jehoahaz at the earliest and more
probably by Jehoash, that Israel and Judah are again in a position
even to attempt excursions into Transjordania.

The earliest likely date for the Moabite war, therefore, is the reign of
Jehoash of Israel (acc. 799/8), with either Joash of Judah (died 797/6) or
his son Amaziah[39] as the Judaean king concerned. The *terminus ad quem*
is Amaziah's attack on Edom (II Kings 14.7) and his foolish challenge to
Israel (II Kings 14.8f), when Jehoash was still king in Israel (died 784/3). So
the Moabite campaign can probably be dated between 799 and 783; if
Amos is referring to the king of Moab's sacrifice of his son *or* to an
atrocity committed during reprisals against Edom, this would be the most
likely period. We must now add, of course, that he may have some quite
different incident in mind; if so, we do not know when it occurred.

Conclusion

Our conclusions in this chapter are chiefly negative. There is no hope of
dating the events Amos refers to with anything approaching certainty. So
long as we are looking for a single period to which to ascribe them all, we
can at best say that a fairly recent date is likelier than an early one; but
once this presupposition is given up, there is little to force our hand. The
very obscurity of the crimes might argue recent occurrences; topical references are often harder to identify than traditional examples. But only
a priori suppositions about the nature of these oracles can yield a firm
dating; the dating cannot, then, itself be used as the basis for any interpretation. As will be seen, our own explanation of the oracles is compatible
with any dating.

Most commentators agree[1] that these oracles build up to a climax in the oracle against Israel, and that the prophet's intention is to startle his hearers by suddenly turning on them after lulling them into a false sense of their own security by denouncing their neighbours. But since it is essential to our interpretation of Amos's teaching that this should be so, this chapter will examine the case for it briefly.

There are two points to be made in favour of the 'climax' view.

(1) As Weiser argued at length in his classic study, it simply makes eminently good sense of this peculiar combination of attacks on foreign nations and on the prophet's own people. It is difficult to think that he would have juxtaposed the two sorts of denunciation without having any special purpose in doing so, for the denunciation of foreigners almost inevitably has a soothing effect on those at home,[2] and it is hard to imagine that Amos was not aware that the Israel oracle would rudely reverse this.

(2) It is consonant with what we know of Amos's method from elsewhere in the book.

(a) In 3.2 we have, in the opinion of most commentators, a saying either actually used by the people[3] or alleged by Amos to be a fair summary of their attitude: 'Only us has Yahweh known of all the families of the earth – therefore he will forgive us all our iniquities.' The prophet cites it as though about to endorse it, and then gives it a twist and rejects it: 'You alone have I known of all the families of the earth – therefore I will punish you for all your iniquities.' Not only the technique, but the point made is the same as in chapters 1 and 2: apparent privilege in fact entails responsibility; Israel is even worse than the admittedly ungodly nations whom she presumes to despise.

(b) In 7.1-9 we have what again is surely a deliberately composed sequence of three visions. In the first two, Amos intercedes against the threatened destruction of Israel and prevails, only to hear God's word of irrevocable doom in the third. Now of course several interpretations are possible. One could argue, with Würthwein,[4] that for a certain period Amos was a *Heilsnabi* and honestly thought that Israel could be saved, but later (in the third vision) came to see that there was no hope left. This might be supported by pointing out that the literary form of the three visions is not identical. But it is surely an attractive hypothesis that Amos, in recounting his inaugural visions, shows how he was disabused of any hopes he had for the people's safety by being allowed to pray for them successfully twice, and hearing them finally condemned only after he himself had been convinced that they had been given every chance.[5] At all events the pattern of hope held out temptingly only to be more cruelly withdrawn is certainly present as the text now stands.

(c) The much-discussed passage at 9.7b embodies the same approach. Wolff is no doubt right in taking 'Did I not bring up Israel from the land of Egypt?' as a further *Zitat*.[6] Amos repeats the people's confession of faith with approval, and then instantly neutralises it - '*and* the Philistines from Caphtor, *and* the Syrians from Kir'. When everyone is somebody, then no one's anybody. Again the rug is pulled out from under the audience's feet.

It is interesting that this technique does not occur in Amos's contemporary Hosea, though it arguably is used by Isaiah, in the Song of the Vineyard (Isaiah 5.1–7), where the prophet's hearers are made to condemn themselves unwittingly in vv.3–4 and only identified as the subjects of the parable in v.7.[1] The classic Old Testament example is, of course, Nathan's parable (II Samuel 12). Its use by Amos is simply one more example of his literary skill and intellectual expertise, which may be added to the other instances which are adduced to prove his affinities with the so-called 'wisdom tradition'.[8] We are not at all concerned to support this conclusion, but simply to agree that Amos does emerge as an intellectual, whose ability to use literary tricks is not surprising.

But various objections can be raised to this interpretation of these chapters:

(i) Würthwein takes much the same line over chapters 1 and 2 as over chapter 7: that they represent a revision by the mature Amos of his earlier work. Integral to this understanding of the prophet is a belief that he began life as a 'cultic' prophet, and that the function of such prophets was to foretell victory for Israel and defeat for her enemies - a view we have already examined. The oracles against the nations, then, are really an indirect prediction of deliverance for Israel by means of a denunciation of her enemies, and when the prophet delivered them he believed in them as such - he was simply doing his job as a cult prophet. Later he came to see that Israel, too, was doomed, but in adding the Israel oracle he was not constructing a coherent literary whole, but simply cancelling his earlier view.

Würthwein's interpretation assumes that Amos began life as a professional cult prophet, a view that is not so popular as it was.[9] But even on its own terms it does not square comfortably with the text. As we have tried to show, the oracles against the nations cannot easily be taken as a denunciation of Israel's enemies, if by that is meant nations with whom she was now at war, nor are their crimes all anti-Israelite. At best we can speak of oracles against Israel's *traditional* enemies; there is no implication that the oracles are an effective means of securing Israel's victory over them.[10] Nor is there any reason to suppose that Amos later renounced his belief that the nations deserved and would receive punishment for their sins. This means that only an alleged unspoken implication – the victory of Israel – is reversed by the addition of the Israel oracle; and if we do not find the implication there anyway, then Würthwein's case falls to the ground.[11]

(ii) Another 'cultic' interpretation of Amos which also rules out any element of surprise in the Israel oracle is Bentzen's theory already discussed.[12] So far from arguing for a complete break after the oracles against the nations, he supposes that the execration of both foreign nations and Israelites was a normal procedure during the autumn festival, and that neither sort of oracle could be expected to occasion any particular surprise. It may be noted that even Kapelrud, who accepts Bentzen's reconstruction in the main, is concerned to dissociate himself from this conclusion, suggesting that denunciation of Israel as a whole for its sins goes far beyond anything that could have formed part of a regular ritual pattern.[13] As we have seen, Wolff regards this as a fundamental weakness in Bentzen's whole case, which destroys the similarity to Egyptian execration texts on which the theory rests.

So we may reasonably conclude that the 'climax' interpretation of these chapters is as likely as any, and that none of the alternatives can easily be made good.

CHAPTER 6

A number of commentators have discussed the basis for Amos's condemnation of atrocities in these chapters, and their suggested answers can be conveniently classified under four headings.

1. *Nationalism and Covenant*
   The nations are denounced for opposing Israel, Yahweh's chosen covenant-people.

2. *Logical extension*
   The moral obligations which Israel is *known* to owe to Yahweh are supposed by extension to apply also to the nations.

3. *Universal law*
   All nations, Israel included, are subject to a divine law which derives from Yahweh's dominion over all mankind.

4. *International customary law*
   The nations are condemned for infringing customs of war accepted or believed to be accepted by all civilised nations.

It is the fourth of these lines of interpretation that we wish to develop and clarify; but first it will be proper to discuss the other three.

1. Nationalism and Covenant

We have already dealt with the main lines of 'nationalistic' interpretations in chapters 2 and 4. Its main proponents are those who think in terms of a cultic *Sitz im Leben* for Amos's oracles, and who maintain that the prophet's function is to denounce the enemies of Israel and so ensure her victory over them when they assail her. So far as the cultic setting is concerned, our comments on Würthwein[1] will suffice. But the nationalistic interpretation is continued by Haran, who regards the only alternative as 'ethical monotheism', which he thinks an unacceptable understanding of Amos:

> It is . . . difficult to agree with the opinion prevailing in commentaries on Amos to the effect that a new theological concept finds expression here: God is supposedly regarded as the national sovereign of Israel alone, yet has already come to make moral demands (thus far moral, not cultic) upon other nations as well. Accordingly, Amos is elevated to the role of progenitor of moral monotheism as against the mono-latry or national henotheism typical of his contemporaries. . . . In actual fact, the demands are national rather than moral in nature and the major part of this prophecy is designed according to the older nationalistic pattern.[2]

But our survey of the historical circumstances has made it clear that, with the possible exception of Aram, if we follow Wolff in seeing 1.3-5 as a reference to very recent atrocities, the threat to Israel from the nations mentioned was largely past in Amos's day, so that we can at best speak of traditional enemies. The oracle on the Philistines need not be concerned with a crime against Israel, and that on Moab almost certainly is not: there is not much cogency in Würthwein's attempt to justify the inclusion of the burning of the king of Edom's bones among anti-Israelite crimes on the dual grounds that (i) Edom was a 'brother' to Israel[3] and (ii) 'hier handelt es um ein Verbrechen von besonderer Ungeheuerlichkeit' – this is just special pleading. The nationalist interpretation does not seem to do justice to Amos's thought.

Weiser also thinks that the source of the moral norms to which Amos is appealing is to be found in nationalist sentiments: 'Der Boden, auf dem der Prophet sich dabei bewegt, liegt nicht über dem Niveau der nationalen Volksreligion.'[4] He uses this point, however, in order to argue that Amos's originality cannot be located in a discovery that the nations, like Israel, stand under God's moral authority, which is what we shall also be con-cerned to argue – not to suggest that Amos endorsed the crude nationalist feelings of his day. The difficulty about Weiser's view, nonetheless, is that it assumes the condemnation of atrocities in war formed part of a folk mythology about the character of Israel's enemies, whereas the fact, already mentioned, that the identity of the victim of atrocities seems to be irrele-vant seems to us rather to suggest that condemnation of atrocities belongs in a broader, more generally humanitarian tradition. It seems that Weiser is likely to be right in stressing that the moral convictions underlying Amos 1.3-2.5 were common to the prophet and his audience, but mistaken in thinking that they derive from a narrow nationalism.

2. Logical extension

But if we reject the line of interpretation that would see opposition to Israel as the essence of the nations' sin, we may still hold that Israel is somehow seen as the focus of moral obligation. For a prophet acquainted, as Amos clearly is, with the convention that Israel owes a special obligation to Yahweh as his chosen people, it might seem to follow that any moral principles binding outside Israel will be so by extension from those known within the covenant relationship. It is not that Israel and the nations share a common covenantal relationship with God; rather, Amos asserts that the ethical obligation incumbent upon Israel is to be seen as binding also on the nations: a startling innovation, so far at least as the popular mind of his day was concerned. Like the cultic view already discussed this is basically Israel-centred in its emphasis. It has the advantage of safeguarding the centrality of God's dealings with Israel, and more particularly of the covenant relationship, in the Old Testament: which is an understandable preoccupation of some scholars. Certainly any interpretation which appears to ignore the importance of the covenant has to make headway against much substantial evidence and theorising. Thus Fensham writes:

> The important trend of thought was that maledictions against a disobedient people shall overtake them, because they have breached the covenant. Calamities predicted against foreign nations must have developed out of these maledictions.[5]

Clements[6] comes to substantially the same conclusions about the prophetic denunciation of Israel's enemies: they always derive from the covenant-ethic, by extension. The nations are assumed to be under ethical obligations because Israel is known to be, in the covenant: compare I Kings 17.18 for an example of this process. Mays[7] is otherwise ready to recognise non-covenantal ethics in Amos, but he still feels that the covenant relationship is primary, the obligation on the nations a secondary extension:

> Amos specifies the basis of Israel's responsibility to Yahweh in 3.2, the election of Israel ... Amos sees Yahweh as the sovereign of history who moves nations in their national careers and can remove them to their earlier spheres (1.5). By analogy with Yahweh's relation to Israel, that sovereignty in the nations' history furnishes the foundation for their responsibility to him.

But it seems to me that, if we accept the 'climax' view of the structure of these chapters, whereby the condemnation of Israel comes as a surprise, we shall have to allow for a less Israel-centred view of ethics than is compatible with such a theory of extension. Amos's hearers are not surprised that foreign nations should be condemned for their atrocities: what startles them is that Israel should be included under the same condemnation. Weiser presents this point with the utmost clarity: the oracles against the nations, he maintains, 'sagen nichts, was den Hörern innerlich fremd ist, sondern enthalten Elemente des Volksglaubens und der Volkshoffnung'.[8] This strongly suggests that the process of extension works in exactly the opposite direction. That war crimes such as foreigners commit are displeasing to Yahweh and will be punished is a commonplace, obvious to all the prophet's audience: much less obvious is the guilt of Israel, for her election by Yahweh has been taken to excuse her from any stringent moral claims upon her, and to preclude any possibility of divine vengeance. She is not subject to the restrictions that bring the rest of mankind before God's judgment seat. Amos's preaching, then, is designed to bring home that Israel must be judged on the same terms (even if by different laws) as her neighbours, and with equal impartiality. Unless something like that is the correct interpretation of Amos's oracles, the possibility of surprise in the Israel oracle is excluded: indeed, it would be the only oracle that would occasion none.[9] The moral obligations owed by foreign nations must be not less but more evident than those imposed on Israel, if these chapters are to serve their purpose. And so we must reject any interpretation that sees such universal morality as deriving from, rather than as presupposed by, the special moral response demanded of the covenant-people.[10]

3. Universal law

If the validity of moral rules governing the conduct of the nations is in fact presupposed by Amos, then it will follow that he is invoking ethical principles common, or supposed by him to be common, to all mankind. Generally the commentators who have thought along these lines have analysed the basis for such an assumption in terms of a universal divine law: something parallel or analogous to the law of Yahweh known in Israel, though not (as we have seen) actually derived from it or identified with it. It is often supposed to stem from the authority of God as the controller of human history;[11] and it is sometimes actually called 'international law', but in the sense not of an internationally agreed code, but of the divine, revealed law obligatory for all mankind whether or not they accept it.[12] Lindblom states the principle clearly; '[the nations] are condemned because of their wickedness and cruelty as such, because of the fact that they have offended against the holy will of Yahweh, which is valid for all peoples'.[13] According to him, this derives from Amos's virtual 'ethical monotheism': Yahweh as the God of the whole universe makes demands on all mankind, not just on his chosen people.[14]

Now this certainly makes better sense than the interpretation in terms of logical extension from the covenant-law; but it still seems to me basically unsatisfactory. If we say that the humanitarian principles the nations are condemned for flouting are part of the divine law, we still run the risk of suggesting that they are condemned for breaking an edict they were unaware of: for what reason was there to think that God's will had been revealed to them? In other words, we shall seem to accuse Amos of irrationality if we hold that he appealed to a supposed divine law; and even if we like to say that he was *not* rational (if that means 'sweetly reasonable'), this interpretation has the serious flaw that it seems to contradict what, according to our arguments so far, Amos was actually trying to do. He is precisely not saying that the nations will perish because they have – all unwittingly, for all he knows – broken the decree of Yahweh; he is saying that they deserve punishment for contravening moral principles which even they should have recognised. The parallel with Israel makes this clear, for the essence of his attack on her is that she, too, should have known better. There seems no escape from the conclusion that Amos thought the foreign nations were infringing humanitarian principles whose force they themselves appreciated; and if that is so, we can call these principles 'God's law' only in an attenuated sense. Either 'God' will have to be understood to mean not 'Yahweh' but 'whatever ultimate principle or force the nation in question recognises', 'their own ultimate religious sanction'; and this is perhaps the interpretation that would be accepted by those who stress the prophet's indebtedness to the international 'wisdom' tradition. Or we shall have to understand 'God's law' to mean a law which God enforces, rather than one which he enacts; and in that case the 'law' is not theological in its roots, only in its application. This is the interpretation we shall be defending, under the next heading.

4. International customary law

In the oracles against the nations, we suggest, God steps in to punish the nations because they are guilty of various atrocities, infringements of supposedly universal moral norms. But the question of the source of these norms is not discussed. They are thought of as part of the common moral sense of all right-minded men: that God shares this moral sense is taken for granted, since he is the very epitome of right-mindedness. But there is no real suggestion that the rightness of the moral norms actually derives from him. Thus the principles at stake in these oracles are essentially part of a conventional morality, which God is assumed to back up with fiery sanctions, rather than actual laws supposed to be issued by him for all the nations of the world to observe. This helps, I would suggest, to make clear the essential rationality of Amos's approach. Israel's neighbours are not denounced for sins which they could not have been expected to recognise as such (e.g. idolatry), but for offences against common humanity; not for disobedience to God, but for failing to follow the dictates of their own moral sense.

Not many of the older scholars regarded Amos 1 and 2 in precisely this light. Humbert came near to it in speaking of 'un Dieu garant d'une morale universelle', and of 'lois élémentaires de la morale humaine'.[15] More recently, however, hints have been thrown out in this direction. Gehman discusses what he calls 'natural law' in the Old Testament, and includes some examples of conventional morality,[16] seeing Amos's oracles as one of the clearest cases: 'these nations outside Israel had violated the common or basic laws concerning the sacredness of human personality . . . It was accordingly recognised and taken for granted that there are certain basic laws and customs which apply to all humanity and that the breaking of them is a transgression against God.'[17]

I have for convenience dubbed this 'international customary law', but an important distinction must be drawn. These conventions are called customary because they are clearly not the subject of explicit legislation, and 'international' because they are concerned with conduct between independent nations in time of war. It has been maintained that they represent a code of conduct actually observed or at least endorsed by the peoples mentioned: thus Max Weber speaks in this connection of 'a form of international religious law which was presupposed as valid among Palestine peoples',[18] and G. H. Jones maintains that 'it is suggested that there was an accepted norm of international behaviour in the ancient Near East, and that some actions would be regarded as atrocious against the background of this common ethos'.[19] Now the existence of such a 'common ethos' is plainly possible, and in the appendix we examine some of the evidence for it; but the argument does not require it. Amos clearly implies that the nations ought ideally to recognise the moral norms which they are transgressing, but it does not follow that they in fact did so. Even if it could be shown that such conventions did not exist outside Israel, Amos's condemnation would not thereby be rendered unreasonable, for the nations' failure even to recognise conventions of 'civilised' conduct might itself be part of the sin condemned. All that follows is that Amos held certain norms of international conduct to be both valid and obviously valid, and that he thought his Israelite audience was likely to agree with him. Our point is that he is appealing not to revealed law, but to conventional or customary law; but it is possible (though in fact we may think it is unlikely) that the 'customs' to which he appealed would not in fact have been accepted outside Israel, or even that not everyone in Israel would have seen the force of them. People do not always recognise the obvious. Consequently we may well be cautious of assuming that Amos is appealing to a 'common ethos': at most it is an ethos which he thought ought to be common.

CHAPTER 7

In this chapter we revert to the six theses we set out in the outline argument and attempt to form some idea of popular notions of morality, divine judgment, and the role of the prophet; then we examine the question of Amos's distinctiveness and originality.

1. Popular belief

Our discussion of conventions of international conduct has already produced examples of popular belief about actual moral norms in this area, and there is nothing to add here. We have assumed throughout that Amos expected his hearers to share his outrage at such atrocities as he mentions, and that having thus awakened their moral sense he could turn it against them by leading them to self-condemnation. But, as we tried to suggest in our initial argument, a number of other conclusions may be drawn about the attitude of Amos's audience, always supposing him to have read their mood correctly. First, and most obviously, they must have believed that sin called down divine punishment. This may seem so trite as not to be worth saying, but it is useful as ruling out certain popular presentations of the prophets as almost the inventors of ethics. Probably no serious scholar now holds this: the awareness that in this as in so much else the prophets depend on a long and widely accepted tradition is one of the very solid gains in modern Old Testament study. But sometimes the moral insensitivity of the people at large in Amos's day is still alleged in a rather extreme form, as though all sense of connection between God and morality and all capacity for moral outrage had drained away from the sink of corruption that Israel under Jeroboam II had become.

In this context it may still be worth stressing that Amos is not preaching into a total vacuum, but assuming that his hearers have some awareness of moral principles and some conviction that God punishes sin with physical disaster, and so that he has some foundation on which to build.

Secondly, Amos's hearers must be supposed to have regarded the nations as moral agents answerable for their conduct. Again, this is really obvious, and it may be doubted whether any culture could be found where members of other nations were regarded as morally unaccountable. But it is perhaps not always seen that this fact renders some interpretations of the work of the prophets rather suspect. We have discussed a number of interpretations of the oracles against the nations in which Amos is seen as extending the scope of moral obligation from Israel to the nations, the most recent being that of Mays: 'By analogy with Yahweh's relation to Israel, that sovereignty in the nations' history furnishes the foundation for their responsibility to him'[1] – and we have argued that the conviction of the nations' moral obligations must on the contrary long antedate Amos. This is not necessarily to say that such obligations were seen as owed to Yahweh in any simple sense; of their supposed basis, if any, we know nothing. But the oracles against the nations must imply that Yahweh was seen as the avenger of acts that infringed the norms of conduct demanded of non-Israelites, and if we may press the Moab oracle this would appear to be so even when the crime in question was not directed against Israel. It seems fair to conclude that the scope both of moral accountability and of Yahweh's power to avenge sin and hence to determine the fortunes of nations was popularly held to extend well beyond Israel by Amos's day: which rules out any attempt to find the prophet's originality in any tendency to ethical universalism or to an extension of Yahweh's power and authority. Weiser makes this point.

Tatsächlich liegen die Dinge ... so, daß die Hörer mit dem, was über die Feinde gesagt wird, einverstanden sind; dann ist aber auch die sittliche Motivierung der Strafe ein Gedanke, der bei ihnen vorausgesetzt werden muß.[2]

Again, I do not wish to suggest that such a view is particularly widespread among recent students of Amos, but simply to stress that in any attempt to reconstruct what 'Israel' believed before the rise of the prophets we must be careful not to go on tacitly assuming it. It is not clear that Amos is here developing further an insight only partially grasped by his contemporaries: he seems simply to be meeting them on their own ground.

Thirdly, the audience must suppose that Israel had a specially privileged position and hence was indemnified against punishment. This is universally agreed. In 3.2 Amos seems to accept the premise but deny the conclusion; in 9.7, to deny both.

Fourthly, Amos's hearers clearly did not expect prophets to proclaim judgment on Israel. This also is generally agreed.

Fifthly, if the surprise technique is to succeed, we must assume not

that the people were unaware of the largely social obligations whose transgressions Amos condemned, but that they saw these as in no way comparable with the international conventions infringed by the nations. In
other words, the average Israelite reacted much as we probably should to
the suggestion that giving short measure in the market was as bad as (worse
than?) disembowelling pregnant women. It takes some swallowing. There
is therefore meant to be nothing in the least original in Amos's examples
in 1.2–2.3, nothing that people would not have recognised at once with
horror: the surprise is wholly in placing social injustice on a par with such
offences, transferring as it were the horror to commonplace everyday mis-
demeanours which people may have regretted but would mostly shrug off
as the kind of thing that just happens in an imperfect world.

Sixthly, and related to this, it seems in some sense to have been less
obvious that Israelites had mutual obligations as individuals than that
nations ought to observe the conventions of war. This again is rather what
one might expect. Once we leave behind the idea that Israelites were
heavily imbued with a sense of covenant-stipulations as primary to their
moral awareness, and allow more place for custom, convention and common sense, it will not be very surprising to find what Amos seems to have
found: that people's moral sensitivity was more easily alerted by manifest
atrocites abroad than by transgressions of the social order at home, in a
nation prosperous and successful in both trade and war.

To sum up. The popular sentiments which we must suppose to have
been widespread in Israel if Amos's message was to find its mark are these:

> All the nations of the world are bound by certain moral laws and are
> accountable for their conduct; and Yahweh, the god who chose Israel as
> his special people, exercises a vigilant control over the way they act,
> punishing transgressions by causing wars and so destroying sinful
> nations. Hence the fortunes of all nations are in his control, and this
> control is exercised according to ethical criteria. Israel, because of her
> special election, is not subject to the divine judgment, and in any case
> her own sins, such as they are, are never of the same order as those of
> foreign nations, since she does not flout international customs. Her
> national life has all the marks of divine favour, and such disorders as
> society may manifest are quite trifling and easily forgiven.

It will be seen that this reconstruction corresponds in part with traditional
sketches of popular belief in eighth-century Israel and in part with traditional presentations of the message of Amos. Of course it cannot be
proved that it is more than a caricature, but we believe that it does clearly
emerge from what Amos tells us, explicitly or by implication.

2. The originality of Amos

We must not, of course, make the mistake of assuming that Amos's own message can be reconstructed simply by negating the outline just presented of the people's beliefs. Our whole purpose has been to define those areas where he accepts without question the popular beliefs of his day, those where he explicitly contradicts them, and those where he presents new ideas. We have suggested that the notion of international conventions of conduct of which Yahweh acts as a guarantor falls into the first category; while Amos's idea that Israel's election does not indemnify her against punishment for sin is an example of the second. It now remains to look for points at which Amos is actually adopting an original position. Two possible examples suggest themselves.

(a) Amos is original in asserting that social injustices and transgressions of the moral code in Israelite society (perhaps equated with 'the law') have the same moral status as transgressions of the much more 'self-evident' laws of international conduct and of the practice of war. So far from international customary law being somehow assimilated to Israel's covenant-law, Amos seems to think that he adds something to the moral intensity of the (revealed) social norms that hold within Israel by placing them on a par with international custom. E. W. Heaton writes that the discourse in the first two chapters of Amos 'discloses the prophet's fundamental conviction that the moral obligation of which all men are aware (and which in later centuries was called natural law) is identical with the personal will of Israel's god'.[3] On the contrary, it looks as though Amos is saying that the personal will of Israel's god, as it is known in the moral rules that should govern her social life, is as binding and as important as if it were part of the moral obligation of which all men are aware. The novelty would then consist in maintaining, against popular opinion, that social morality (understood as impartiality in justice and care for the rights of the helpless) is not a mere piece of arbitrary divine legislation nor a merely human convention, but almost a part of the order of nature – self-evident to any right-thinking man.

(b) A further novelty, apparently, was Amos's conviction that Israel was not indemnified against punishment but was all the more accountable in view of her election. The argument does not run: since Yahweh has revealed his will to Israel alone, how scrupulous she ought to be in keeping it and therefore how culpable she is if she transgresses it; but rather: since the rightness of the obligations laid on Israel ought to be as obvious as if they were agreed on by all men, how much worse her guilt is when she also has the advantage of a special personal contact with God to endorse them. Amos thus totally reverses the popular idea of election. It becomes simply a factor aggravating still further the deep guilt of Israel, and in the end is apparently to be altogether abrogated by Yahweh.

APPENDIX: International law in the ancient Near East

The purpose of this appendix is to set out a selection of comparative material from the ancient Near East on international conventions, especially those concerned with warfare. The subject deserves a full-length study in its own right, but for our purposes the need is simply to show that the kind of conventions we have supposed Amos to be appealing to are not unattested in the ancient world. In other words, this is meant to serve as a 'feasibility study', not in any way as a 'proof' that our interpretation of Amos is correct.

In this title as throughout the monograph I have spoken of 'international law', and this may be thought unwise, since it is a closely defined concept which lawyers are generally wary of applying outside the context of modern international relations, with properly regulated and enforceable treaties and conventions. Incidentally the same applies to the idea of war crimes, which we have freely referred to; it is arguable that such a category of crime has not been recognised until this century, and of course its exact legal status was one of the major problems attending the Nuremberg trials. International law properly so called may be defined as 'eine rechtliche Ordnung mehrerer selbständig nebeneinander stehender, sich gegenseitig als gleich berechtigt anerkennender und durch einen regelmäßigen Austausch kultureller und wirtschaftlicher Art verbundener Staaten'.[1] Older writers on international law, so far as I am able to judge, saw nothing approximating to this in antiquity before some very rudimentary beginnings in classical Greece and Rome.[2] More recently, however, with the publication of an increasing number of treaties from the ancient Near East, this judgment has had to be modified, at least by orientalists; professional international lawyers have also altered their assessment of the origins of international law, though so far at least as standard text-books are concerned this seems to have meant only the rather grudging addition of a few pages on pre-classical antiquity rather than any more full-blown treatment, so that we have little professional help available in studying the field. The only extensive study of international law in the ancient Near

East that I can find which is really relevant to our concern is that of
Preiser, quoted above; so I shall draw very heavily on him.

We must not, however, limit ourselves entirely to 'international law' in
the strict sense defined above – agreed codes of international conduct, confirmed by treaty. We shall also need to look at accepted international
conventions of diplomacy and war, and also at those kinds of conduct in
international affairs to which nations regarded themselves and others as
constrained, regardless of whether anyone but themselves in fact accepted
them. In this way we may hope to cover the field of possible parallels to
Amos 1.3–2.3. We may divide the subject thus:

1. International law proper – treaties etc.
2. Agreed international conventions not legally ratified.
3. Unilaterally accepted norms of international conduct.

1. International law proper

Preiser has studied the evidence for the existence of international law properly so called in the ancient Near East, and has come to the conclusion
that our only evidence for it is to be found in roughly the period from the
beginning of the fifteenth to the end of the thirteenth centuries. Before
this, the only suggestion of anything like international law is to be found
in the protracted boundary-dispute between the city-states of Lagash and
Umma, at the start of the third millennium, in the course of which the
king of Kish at one point acted as mediator, setting up a boundary-stone
and binding both parties to observe the border thus defined.[3] But the
details of this transaction are very unclear, and there is some reason to
think that the king of Kish was in the position of overlord to the rulers of
Lagash and Umma, so that no question of strictly international relations
arises.[4] The clearest examples of international law in the usual sense will
naturally appear in the so-called parity treaties between major powers,
where there is no question of vassalage. The most famous of these, and the
only one extant among the Hittite treaties, is between Rameses II and
Hattusilis III.[5] Apart from being, as would be expected, a pact of mutual
non-aggression, it includes also a promise of military aid in the event of
rebellion by the vassals of either party, a mutual obligation to ensure the
succession, and an extradition treaty. It is not altogether clear whether
this is meant to apply just to political prisoners who have escaped, or
rather to all who leave one country for the other without permission from
their own king: Mettgenberg[6] argues that the treaty is designed to make
emigration in itself a crime, probably because of its possible harmful effect
on the labour forces of both states involved. Very interesting from our
point of view is the provision that various specified punishments, in par-

ticular mutilation, may not be carried out on any man so extradited, or on his family;[7] these rules are reminiscent of our principle of refusing extradition to a state whose standards of justice or methods of punishment are not acceptable to us.

The only other parity treaty that demands consideration is that between Niqmepa, king of Mukish and Alalakh, and Ir-IM, king of Tunip, preserved on the second of the Alalakh tablets. This provides for the extradition of marauders for judgment by their own king:

(55) If someone of my territory shall have entered into your territory for banditry (?)

(56) you shall surely not keep them as though they were of your land, you shall surely

(57) not detain them within your territory but must return them to my territory.

(58) You must round them up and return them to my territory.[8]

But unlike the Rameses–Hattusilis treaty it explicitly provides that escaped prisoners may be granted asylum if they succeed in fleeing from one state to the other:

(20) If a prisoner of my country escapes to your country then he verily free [sic].

(21) and if the prisoner has been freed you may neither seize (him) nor (return him to me).[9]

In the event of a citizen who is not a prisoner fleeing for asylum, his king must be informed;[10] but the tablet is damaged, and it is not possible to say whether any further steps were to be taken.

Whether one can speak of international law in vassal treaties, it is harder to say. In modern terms one could not: but the line between parity and vassal treaties in the Near East is not hard and fast; as Korošec's analysis shows, a parity treaty is formally no more than a mutual vassal treaty, and 'vassalage' is a very fluid idea, ranging from complete subjugation to merely nominal inferiority.[11] In the absence of any theoretically formulated concept of international law the borderline between this and 'state' law will hardly be closely definable, and some legal provisions are bound to fall on both sides of it.[12] For our purposes it does not much matter exactly how far we allow vassal treaties to contain international law: certainly some of them have provisions which approach closely to it. The treaty between Suppiluliumas and Mattiwaza of Mitanni[13] is formally a vassal treaty; but the Hittite king lays emphasis, in the preamble which explains why his vassal should be willing to obey him, on the fact that while the Hittites have made war on many neighbouring peoples, they have never infringed the sovereignty of Mitanni by removing so much as a reed or a twig. The obligation to extradition again applies, though naturally enough it is unilateral.[14] Mattiwaza must extradite any fugitives from Hatti, while Suppiluliumas may grant asylum to Mitannian fugitives at his discretion.

The Sefire treaties also contain provisions similar to those of the Rameses-Hattusilis treaty discussed above;[15] thus in Sefire III[16] Mati'el is to hand over all who plot against Bir-Ga'yah, the overlord, as well as fugitives from justice; he has a duty to help maintain the succession, and his own is in turn guaranteed; he must allow Bir-Ga'yah's ambassadors to pass unhindered, and refrain from participating in any plots against his household, and if necessary avenge his assassination; and both partners must respect each other's territorial rights, though the vassal's rights are of course ultimately subordinate to his overlord's. Apparently the treaty also envisages mutual extradition pacts between Bir-Ga'yah and the (? sovereign) states around him - thus:

> And as for the (k)ings of (my vicin)ity, if a fugitive of mine flees to one of them, and a fugitive of theirs flees and comes to me, if he has restored mine, I shall return (his; and) you yourself shall (no)t try to hinder me.[17]

2. Agreed international conventions not legally ratified

If so much 'international law' can be gleaned from legally ratified treaties, there is a much larger area of international agreement on matters not specially codified, but necessary if peaceful relations are to be preserved between states. One such matter that has already arisen, in Sefire III, is the question of ambassadors. Wherever Egyptian influence prevailed in the second millennium, the obligation to respect the person of the ambassador might be taken for granted. Thus Amarna letter no. 30[18] preserves a passport for an ambassador passing through Palestine. Letters 7 and 8 demand vengeance for attacks on properly accredited ambassadors: in letter 8 Amenophis IV is asked by Burraburiash to punish the inhabitants of Canaan (Kinaḫḫi), where his ambassadors have been set upon and either killed or subjected to various atrocities (one man's feet have been cut off, another has been stood on his head). Disrespect of any kind for ambassadors is felt as an insult: thus in letter 3 a Babylonian prince complains that the Pharaoh (Amenophis III) has kept his ambassadors waiting for six years without granting them an audience and without making proper provision for their needs. Again, Tushratta writes angrily to Amenophis IV because his envoys have not been allowed to return home; he threatens that he will himself retain the Egyptian ambassadors as hostages until his own are restored to him.

It seems probable that the conventions on diplomatic missions of the Amarna age are the final flowering of a continuous tradition going back to the turn of the second millennium. The evidence of the Mari letters, as discussed by Miss Munn-Rankin,[19] suggests that such conventions were already commonplace in Mesopotamia by the eighteenth century, though in a less highly developed form. There is less immunity for ambassadors than in the Egyptian texts: thus Zimri-lim's envoy is obliged to stay at Hammurabi's court until given permission to leave, even though he has been recalled;[20] and officials – though not private individuals – may detain envoys before they reach the court if their visit at that time is judged to be inopportune.[21] On the other hand, diplomatic missions were probably exempt from customs dues,[22] and there were elaborate codes dictating the safe conduct of ambassadors returning home, who had to be accompanied by a native of the country to which they had been accredited, not just to the border but all the way back to their own court.[23] Sending back ambassadors without such an escort is a calculated affront.[24] From a later age, there is independent evidence of the respect in which ambassadors were held in the ancient Near East in II Samuel 10.4, where the Ammonites' contempt for David's legation leads to war.

There is good reason to think that the conventions of diplomacy extended beyond such basic provisions to include a careful regulation of the niceties of official procedure. This has been the subject of a study by J. Pirenne,[25] and there is also evidence from Mari.[26] Among the complaints about finer points of protocol in the Amarna letters is one from Suppiluliumas, who writes to Amenophis IV to upbraid him for reversing the accepted order of names in the greeting at the head of a letter, placing his own name before that of the addressee.[27] One cannot tell whether this was a deliberately contrived snub, or simply a careless mistake by an official: but it is clearly a matter that could strain international relations. Failure to observe the accustomed protocol always requires explanation. Thus the king of Alasia apologises abjectly for his failure to send a delegation to an Egyptian festival – he did not know it was to be celebrated.[28] None of these conventions, we may suppose, was a matter for formal, legal agreement; rather they are simply accepted norms of international diplomatic courtesy.

But there is also evidence of widespread agreement that certain acts of a more serious kind were unacceptable and deserving of censure and/or punishment. In some cases one can hardly imagine a civilised society that would not so regard them: e.g. the assassination of rulers,[29] the plundering of innocent towns,[30] wholesale massacre.[31] There are other offences which the peoples of the ancient Near East thought of as extremely grave, hedging them about with dire curses, which the modern world regards with rather less severity: such are especially the infringement of boundary-rights[32] – though this may include the infringement of national sovereignty – and disturbing the dead. This second crime is a commonplace. There are numerous examples in the texts collected by Donner and Röllig, e.g.

> Sarkophag, welchen (')TB'L, Sohn des 'ḤRM, König von Byblos, für 'ḤRM, seinen Vater, anfertigte, als er ihn in der Ewigkeit wiederlegte. *Wenn aber* (?) ein König unter den Königen oder ein Statthalter unter den Statthaltern oder der Befehlshaber eines Lagers gegen Byblos heraufgezogen ist und diesen Sarkophag aufdeckt, dann soll der Stab seiner Herrschaft entblättert werden, soll sein Königsthron umgestürzt werden und der Friede soll weichen von Byblos. (*c.* 1000 B.C.)[33]

This sort of attitude one may suppose to lie behind Amos 2.1-3. In the same category belongs cannibalism: how heinous a crime it was held to be may be seen from its use as an ultimate curse in Esarhaddon's vassal treaties: thus

> As the dismembered flesh of her young is put in the mouth of the ewe, just so may they make you eat the flesh of your women, your brothers, your sons, and your daughters.[34]

Before we pass on to consider unilaterally held views on international conduct, we may mention a couple of other issues which appear to be taken as matters of universal agreement, though one cannot be quite sure. A recurring complaint in the Amarna letters is that the Egyptian official's children have been handed over to the enemy, possibly as hostages, or else as slaves, by way of tribute – thus e.g.

> Dahin sind unsere Söhne (und unsere) Töchter neb(s)t uns selbst, indem sie gegeben worden sind in Iarimuta für die Ret(tu)ng unseres Lebens.[35]

Rib-addi's point may be simply to show the extremity of need to which the Egyptian community has been reduced, and so to summon Pharoah's aid; but it is at least possible that he is protesting against what is felt to be a cruel and illicit way of concluding a truce. We would then be reminded of I Samuel 11.2, where the Ammonites offer peace to the men of Jabesh-gilead on condition that every man's right eye is put out: a condition felt to be so harsh as to contravene the laws of civilised conduct, and consequently to be answered by an immediate declaration of war. It is, we note, the Ammonites who are again seen practising atrocities against Gilead in Amos 1.13-15, where they are accused of ripping open pregnant women. Here we seem definitely to be moving into the sphere of war crimes felt to be such only by particular nations: our third sub-division.

3. Unilaterally accepted norms of international conduct

The atrocity just mentioned is also referred to with abhorrence in II Kings 8.12 and 15.16, and Hosea 13.16: but outside Israel it seems rather to be a normal and accepted practice. Tiglath-pileser I (*c.* 1100) is praised because 'he hacked to pieces the women with child, and pierced the bodies of the weak',[36] and in the *Iliad* Agamemnon persuades Menelaus to harden his heart against the Trojans with the words:[37]

$$... τῶν μή τις ὑπεκφύγοι αἰπὺν ὄλεθρον$$
$$χεῖράς θ' ἡμετέρας, μηδ' ὅν τινα γαστέρι μήτηρ$$
$$κοῦρον ἐόντα φέροι, μηδ' ὃς φύγοι, ἀλλ' ἅμα πάντες$$
$$Ἰλίου ἐξαπολοίατ' ἀκήδεστοι καὶ ἄφαντοι.$$

This is not to say, of course, that such an outrage was not felt to be very terrible - indeed it obviously serves as a paradigm of the worst destruction possible - but only that it was apparently an accepted feature of ancient warfare, and not forbidden by any 'rules of war', at least in the two instances we have cited. Evidently it was not accepted in Israel, though the law nowhere forbids it; it may also have been rejected by some other nations.

This brings us to a consideration of the rules of war, and here we shall do well not to assume any international agreement. So far as I know there is no evidence to suggest that any formal methods of declaring or waging war were literally agreed among nations of the ancient Near East, and though no doubt there were some conventions governing the smaller details of battles, we have no reason to think of complicated rules of chivalry such as existed in medieval warfare, still less of anything approximating to the Geneva Convention. What does appear, however, is that each nation had its own ideas of what practices it might legitimately indulge in itself, and what it might regard as legitimate in an enemy. As we have just seen, the treatment of pregnant women during an invasion was viewed differently by Israelites and Assyrians.[38] Prisoners of war also present a problem which each nation solves in its own way. II Kings 6.22 suggests that Israel had some definite rules regarding the treatment to be meted out to such prisoners, though what the rules were is uncertain because of exegetical difficulties. Following the MT, one must probably conclude that 'captured by sword and bow' is a technical term, distinguishing those taken in battle from those who surrender voluntarily; in which case Elisha is appealing to a rule that prisoners of war who surrender are not to be executed, and arguing that *a fortiori* those taken by force should be allowed to live.[39] But this argument is an oddity - it would be more convincing if reversed - and in any case these prisoners have been taken by trickery, not in any sense 'by sword and bow': and perhaps, therefore, we should read לֹא with the LXX,[40] and take Elisha to mean that prisoners who have not been taken in fair fight ought not to be executed, since they have not had a chance to defend themselves.[41] This suggests that it was otherwise regular to kill prisoners of war out of hand, which would accord with the religious practice of the ban. There is evidence, however, that in practice mercy might be shown to conquered enemies - cf. I Kings 20.31ff, where indeed v.31 suggests that Israel was known (perhaps in contrast to Assyria) for her humane record in this respect. For other evidence of rules of war in Israel see Deuteronomy 20.10-20; and cf. Joshua 10.24 and Isaiah 51.23 for customs of asserting conquest.

Among the Hittites, too, there is definite evidence of the existence of a code regulating the conduct of war.[42] Hittite rulers, it appears, were no more willing than modern leaders to acknowledge self-aggrandisement and territorial expansion as motives for undertaking war: aggression was theoretically illicit (the contrast with Assyria is striking). Any nation that was to be attacked must therefore first be 'convicted', by a judicial process conducted through diplomatic channels, of some offence against Hatti, and war might then ensue as a divine sentence of execution. The rules for the treatment of prisoners and captured cities are reminiscent of those we have supposed to lie behind II Kings 6.22. A town that holds out against siege must be plundered and burnt down, though the inhabitants must be removed alive and resettled: but in case of surrender the conquering general is empowered to allow the inhabitants to remain after the town has been plundered, annexing them to the Hittite empire and imposing a vassal treaty. In neither case, apparently, might a wholesale massacre of the population be ordered, and in the context of ancient Near Eastern warfare this, like the Hittite laws, suggests that humanitarian considerations weighed more heavily with the Hittites than with most of their neighbours.[43] At all events the Hittite rules of war are a clear example of a unilateral code of international conduct; probably they did not expect other states to observe them, and if they did, they must have been sadly disappointed.

Conclusion

We have now examined some of the evidence for conventions referring to international relations in peace and war, and have found, I believe, enough material to justify our conclusion that Amos refers to some such conventions rather than, say, to divine covenant-law, when condemning the nations for their sin. Perhaps in the light of our threefold classification of the material from ancient Near Eastern sources (though the dividing lines remain somewhat uncertain and fluid) we might briefly attempt a more exact definition of these conventions. We argued that there is not enough evidence to justify the view that Amos is appealing to actual international agreements, rather than to principles of conduct which he believes all nations *ought* to accept - though he may be; and we have seen that some of the material from non-Israelite sources is similarly ambiguous, while there are clearly some rules, especially those relating to the conduct of war, where nations acknowledged different norms, even though each individual state supposed that its own norms had or ought to have a universal validity. In the case of Ammon, we have explicit evidence to suggest that the Ammonites did not recognise any such moral obligations in war as Amos clearly believed they should. In terms of our classification, then, we may remain uncertain whether to assign Amos 1.3–2.3 to class (2) or class (3), but with some inclination towards the latter. It appears, however, that the Tyre and Edom oracles, whose authenticity we have already seen other grounds for doubting, really belong to class (1); for as the studies of Priest and Fishbane have demonstrated, what is here envisaged is the breaking of a treaty rather than the infringement of rules designed to prevent atrocities. Tyre and Edom have failed to remember obligations to which they are contractually committed - obligations of respect for national sovereignty, and non-aggression; the other nations have committed war crimes which have nothing to do with the political or diplomatic relationship in which they stand towards their victims. One cannot claim that Amos could not have mixed the two kinds of accusation in one set of oracles - the division is made mainly for our own convenience, though it does recognise a genuine logical difference - yet perhaps we may allow the distinction to count towards the cumulative argument for excising 1.9–12. With this passage removed, the oracles against the nations present a more coherent picture.

One final note: the connection of the international conventions we have discussed with God or the gods appears in general to be very slight, at least so far as explicit references are concerned. Usually the appeal is simply to the accepted way of doing things (this particularly in issues relating to diplomatic practice), or to some kind of moral sense of what is fitting. Only in treaties regulating international affairs is there special reference to the gods, who act as witnesses to the signing of the treaty and who will, it is hoped, intervene to punish the partner who breaks his promise to keep its terms. They are the guarantors of treaty-obligation, not its source. We have already said that the relationship of Yahweh to the sins of the nations in Amos appears to be that of avenger of guilt, rather than explicitly the source of the moral norms they have infringed: not lawgiver so much as judge. From such ancient Near Eastern evidence as we have been able to survey, this is just what we should expect.

Additional Note: The Hittite rules of war

Most of the evidence for rules of war among the Hittites is to be found in the Annals of Muršiliš.[44] A typical formal declaration of war is as follows:

> Zu Uḫḫa-LÚ-iš aber sandte ich meinen Boten und schrieb ihm: 'Meine Untertanen, die zu dir kamen, als ich die von dir zurückforderte, hast du sie mir nicht zurückgegeben. Und du hast mich ein Kind gescholten, und mich mißachtet. Nun auf denn! Wir werden miteinander kämpfen!
>
> Und der Wettergott, mein Herr, soll unseren Rechtsstreit entscheiden.'[45]

The burning of a town that resists, and the deportation of at least part of the population,[46] is several times recorded.[47] The mercy of the Hittite kings, however, is also frequently attested. They report instances of it with obvious pride, in sharp contrast to the gloating reports of massacre and sophisticated torture familiar from Assyrian sources. Thus Muršiliš relates how he sent an ultimatum to rebellious vassals threatening total devastation; but

> ... wie die Leute von Kammamma und die Leu(te von ... solches) hörten, erschraken (sie und) töteten (den Pazzanaš und den Nunnutaš). Die Leute von Kammamma aber und die L(eute von ...) wurden mir (zum zweiten Male wieder) untertan.[48]

A little further on Muršiliš tells how the inhabitants of a besieged city, worn down by hunger and thirst, came and pleaded with him, and how he transported some of the population but, as a reward for their submission, killed none of them;[49] while in another place he reports an act of mercy which any Assyrian king would have derided:

> ... Aber sowie über mich (Manapa-Dattas hö)rte: 'Der König des Hatti-

Landes kommt', (fürchte)te er sich, und er (kam) mir infolgedessen
nicht entgegen (und) sandte mir seine Mutter, Greise und Greisinnen
(entgegen), und sie kamen (und) (fielen) mir zu Füßen. Und weil mir
die Frauen zu Füßen fielen, willfahrte ich (den Frauen) zuliebe und
zog darauf (nicht) nach dem Šeḫafluß(-land).[50]

Finally we may note Muršiliš's boast that, in taking the land of Ḫurna,
he was careful not to disturb the sanctuary of the storm-god, but allowed
all its officials and votaries to continue as before; and the whole land was
left in peace, under a light tribute.[51]

NOTES

Chapter 1

1 For an important discussion of the principle involved here see C. B. Macpherson, *The Political Theory of Possessive Individualism*, Oxford 1962, especially 6–7.

Chapter 2

1 R. E. Clements, *Prophecy and Tradition*, Oxford 1975, 60–1.

2 N. K. Gottwald, *All the Kingdoms of the Earth*, New York and London 1964.

3 J. H. Hayes, 'The Usage of Oracles against Foreign Nations in Ancient Israel', *JBL* 87 (1968), 81–92.

4 Cf. R. Bach, *Die Aufforderung zur Flucht und zum Kampf im alttesta-mentlichen Prophetenspruch*, WMANT 9, 1962.

5 On taunts against individuals see R. de Vaux, 'Single Combat in the Old Testament' in *The Bible and the Ancient Near East*, London 1972, 122–35.

6 Gottwald, *op. cit.*, 48; see his note 14 for bibliography.

7 Which, however, need not be intended to be heard by him: it may be a 'word of power', cf. G. Fohrer, 'Prophetie und Magie' in *Studien zur alttestamentlichen Prophetie (1949–65)*, BZAW 99, 1967, 242–64 (reprinted from *ZAW* 78 (1966)); cf. also Clements, *Prophecy and Tradition*, 62.

8 See Gottwald, *op. cit.*, 47–50; W. F. Albright, 'The Oracles of Balaam', *JBL* 63 (1944), 207–33; F. M. Cross and D. N. Freedman, 'The Blessing of Moses', *JBL* 67 (1948), 191–210, for further discussion of the linguistic and orthographical criteria involved.

9 See especially G. von Rad, *Der heilige Krieg im alten Israel*, Zurich 1951, and *Old Testament Theology*, vol. II, London 1965, 159ff; E. Würthwein, 'Jesaja 7, 1–9. Ein Beitrag zu dem Thema "Prophetie und Politik"' in *Theologie als Glaubenswagnis* (Festschrift for Karl Heim), Tübingen and Hamburg 1954, 47–63; R. Bach, *op. cit.*; H. Wildberger, '"Glauben" im Alten Testament', *ZThK* 65 (1968), 129–59.

10 See, inter alia, G. Dossin, 'Sur le prophétisme à Mari' in *La divination en Mésopotamie ancienne et dans les régions voisines* (14e rencontre assyrio-logique internationale, Strasbourg 2–6 July 1965), Paris 1966, 77–86; F. Ellermeier, *Prophetie in Mari und Israel*, Theologische und orienta-lische Arbeiten 1, Hertzberg 1968; A. Malamat, 'Prophetic Revelations in

New Documents from Mari and the Bible', *VTS* 15 (1966), 214-19; W. L. Moran, 'New Evidence from Mari on the History of Prophecy', *Biblica* 50 (1969), 15-56; J. H. Hayes, 'Prophetism at Mari and Old Testament Parallels', *AThR* 49 (1967), 397-409.

11 G. Fohrer, 'Remarks on Modern Interpretations of the Prophets', *JBL* 80 (1961), 309-19.

12 Both arguments are rightly used by Clements, *op. cit.*, 71.

13 This point is well made by Gottwald, *op cit.*, 109-10. But see below, pp. 21 and 40, for attempts to see a crime against Israel here.

14 S. Herrmann, *A History of Israel in Old Testament Times*, London 1975, 233-4, notes recent cautions against the 'Indian summer' or 'lull before the storm' view of the reigns of Jeroboam II and Uzziah: nevertheless it remains implausible to think of Israel as surrounded by enemies in this period. See below, chapter 4.

15 Clements, *op. cit.*, 60 and 65.

16 *Ibid.*, 71-2.

17 See F. Stolz, *Interpreting the Old Testament*, London 1975, 60-2, and bibliography there.

18 See S. Mowinckel, *The Psalms in Israel's Worship*, Oxford 1962, vol. I, 217-18, and vol. II, 58-61.

19 See H. J. Kraus, *Psalmen*, BK XV, 1966, *ad loc.*

20 *Ibid., ad loc.*; cf. also J. Begrich, 'Das priesterliche Heilsorakel', *ZAW* 52 (1934), 81-92.

21 E. Würthwein, 'Amosstudien', *ZAW* 62 (1949), 10-52.

22 See J. Gray, *I & II Kings*, OTL, 1964, *ad loc.*; B. S. Childs, *Isaiah and the Assyrian Crisis*, SBTh II.3, 1967, 103.

23 See E. Würthwein, 'Der Ursprung der prophetischen Gerichtsrede' in *Wort und Existenz: Studien zum alten Testament*, Göttingen 1970, 111-28 (= *ZThK* 49 (1952), 1-16). For an exhaustive discussion of the origin of *Gerichtsreden* see E. von Waldow, *Der traditionsgeschichtliche Hintergrund der prophetischen Gerichtsreden*, BZAW 85, 1963.

24 This theory is discussed at length by G. H. Jones in his unpublished Ph.D. dissertation 'An Examination of Some Leading Motifs in the Prophetic Oracles against Foreign Nations', University College of North Wales, Bangor, 1970. He sees as early as Gressmann the implication that 'the oracles against foreign nations pronounce judgment on the nations, which meant salvation for Israel'. He adds: 'That the oracles against foreign nations were intentionally salvation oracles in this way is very unlikely' (p. 4).

25 H. Graf Reventlow, *Das Amt des Propheten bei Amos*, Göttingen 1962; *Wächter Über Israel. Ezechiel und seine Traditionen*, BZAW 82, 1962; *Liturgie und prophetisches Ich bei Jeremia*, Gütersloh 1963.

26 A. Bentzen, 'The Ritual Background of Amos 1.2-2.16', *OS* 8 (1950), 85-99; see also A. S. Kapelrud, *Central Ideas in Amos*, Oslo 1961.

27 See below, pp. 22-4.

28 M. Weiss, 'The Pattern of the "Execration Texts" in the Prophetic Literature', *IEJ* 19 (1969), 150-7.

29 For this point cf. also S. M. Paul, 'Amos 1.3-2.3: A Concatenous Literary Pattern', *JBL* 90 (1971), 397-403. I do not however think that his own

attractive alternative theory of a catchword or cyclic arrangement in the oracles has any more power to tip the scales against the probable deletions discussed in chapter 2.

30 Fohrer, 'Prophetie und Magie', 40–2.
31 Cf. K. Tallquist, *Himmelsgegenden und Winde*, Studia Orientalia 2, Helsinki 1928, 118–19. Weiss (*op cit.*, 156) prefers this to the explanation offered by H. W. Wolff (*Joel and Amos*, Philadelphia 1977, 145–6) – following W. Helck, *Die Beziehungen Ägyptens zu Vorderasien im 3. und 2. Jahrtausend vor Chr.*, Ägyptologische Abhandlungen 5, Wiesbaden 1962, 62–3 – that the order of naming of countries in Egyptian texts follows the major trading routes from Egypt.

 (Note: Wolff, *Joel and Amos* is a translation of the German original, *Dodekapropheton 2: Joel und Amos*, BK XIV, 1969.)

32 See below, p. 38.
33 Wolff, *Joel and Amos*, 145–7.
34 In *Das Amt des Propheten bei Amos*.
35 Gottwald, *op cit.*, 104.
36 See below, p. 25.
37 Gottwald, *op cit.*, 105.
38 *Ibid.* 106
39 Clements, *Prophecy and Tradition*, 65.
40 Wolff, *Joel and Amos*, 138; cf. the same author's *Amos' geistige Heimat*, Neukirchen 1964, 26–9.
41 Cf. W. M. W. Roth, 'The Numerical Sequence x/x + 1 in the Old Testament', *VT* 12 (1962), 300–11, and 'Numerical Sayings in the Old Testament', *VTS* 13 (1965).
42 Gottwald adds another argument, that Amos appears to have been familiar with 'an ancient prophetic scroll which was apparently also employed in Joel 3.16–18'. In this he draws on Y. Kaufmann, *A History of the Religion of Israel* (tr. M. Greenberg), London 1961, III.1, 61–2. But few commentators regard Amos 1.2 as part of the oracles against the nations in any case; frequently it is taken to be inauthentic; and other explanations than a common source are available for the literary connection with Joel.
43 Clements, *op. cit.*, 72.
44 'Die Bedrohung von Feinden mochte man zu jeder Zeit gern hören': author's own translation from Wolff, *Dodekapropheton 2: Joel und Amos*, 181 (see note 31 above); cf. Wolff, *Joel and Amos*, 149.

Chapter 3

1 H. W. Hogg, 'The Starting Point of the Religious Message of Amos' in *Transactions of the 3rd International Congress for the History of Religions*, ed. P. S. Allen and J. de M. Johnson, Oxford 1908, I. 325–7; cited in R. S. Cripps, *A Critical and Exegetical Commentary on the Book of Amos*, 2nd edn, London 1955; cf. K. Budde, 'Zu Text und Auslegung des Buches Amos', *JBL* 43 (1924), 46–131.
2 A. Néher, *Amos*, Paris 1950.
3 J. Morgenstern, 'Amos Studies IV', *HUCA* 32 (1961).

4 Wolff, *Joel and Amos, ad loc.*; A. Weiser, *Das Buch der zwölf kleinen Propheten*, ATD, 1967, *ad loc.*

5 Budde, *op cit.*

6 V. Maag, *Text, Wortschatz und Begriffswelt des Buches Amos*, Leiden 1951, 5.

7 T. H. Robinson, *Die zwölf kleinen Propheten*, HAT, 1938.

8 There is some evidence of links between Phoenicia and Edom as early as the Ras Shamra texts: cf. Keret III.5, where Keret undertakes a journey to *'udm*.

9 W. Nowack, *Die kleinen Propheten*, Göttingen 1897.

10 Weiser, *Das Buch der zwölf kleinen Propheten, ad loc.*

11 W. R. Harper, *Amos and Hosea*, ICC, 1905.

12 E. A. Edghill, *The Book of Amos*, London 1914.

13 Cited *ibid.*

14 VTE 7.545f.

15 See A. Malamat, 'Amos 1.5 in the Light of the Til Barsip Inscriptions', *BASOR* 129 (1953), 25f.

16 M. Haran, 'The Rise and Decline of the Empire of Jeroboam ben Joash', *VT* 17 (1967), 266–97.

17 Gottwald, *All the Kingdoms of the Earth*, 95 (footnote).

18 See J. A. Fitzmyer, *The Aramaic Inscriptions of Sefire*, Biblica et Orientalia 19, Rome 1967; cf. *KAI* 224.2-3.

19 Cf. Deut. 21.10, II Sam. 12.31, and CH 280f (*ANET* 177).

20 M. Fishbane, 'The Treaty Background of Amos 1.11', *JBL* 89 (1970), 313–18. Cf. also J. Priest, 'The Covenant of Brothers', *JBL* 84 (1965), 400–6.

21 If Israel is indeed meant, we may recall II Sam. 5.11 and I Kings 5.15ff. Cripps's suggestion that the covenant thus infringed was between Edom and the state to which the slaves belonged (Israel, he thought) could be right, but does not seem a natural interpretation.

22 Fishbane has since modified his position slightly, and now holds that and *ra'amu* are translation equivalents though deriving ultimately from different Semitic roots: see his 'Additional Remarks on RḤMYW (Amos 1.11)', *JBL* 91 (1972), 391-3. This point about the semantic as opposed to etymological equivalence of the two roots had been made by G. Schmuttermayr, 'RḤM - eine lexikalische Studie', *Biblica* 51 (1970), 499–532.

23 G. R. Driver, 'Linguistic and Textual Problems - Minor Prophets II', *JTS* 39 (1938), 260–73, argues that this crime could have nothing to do with enlarging one's borders, and so that the passage is best understood as 'because they broke through into the plateau' (הרר ' interpreted from an Arabic analogue). Of the atrocity against pregnant women he says 'being an incident in all ancient campaigns, [it] was unlikely to be the subject of a special denunciation by the prophet' - cf. Budde, *op. cit.* This begs a number of questions!

24 Würthwein, 'Amosstudien', 10–52.

25 N. H. Torczyner, *hallason weʰ hassepher*, Jerusalem 1955, II.66.

26 J. R. Bartlett, 'The Moabites and Edomites' in *Peoples of Old Testament*

Times, ed. D. J. Wiseman, Oxford 1973, 228-58 - for this suggestion see note 84 on p. 254.

27 K. Marti, 'Zur Komposition von Amos 1.3-2.3', BZAW 33, 1917, 323-30.

28 H. E. W. Fosbroke, *Amos*, IB VI, New York 1956.

29 J. L. Mays, *Amos*, OTL, 1969.

30 Wolff, *Joel and Amos*, 140-1.

31 Cf. the defences by K. Cramer, *Amos - Versuch einer theologischen Interpretation*, BWANT III.15, 1930; Priest, *op. cit.*; Fishbane, 'The Treaty Background'; M. A. Beek, 'The Religious Background of Amos 2.6-8', *OS* 5 (1948), 132-41; and many of the older commentators.

32 W. Rudolph, 'Die angefochtenen Völkersprüche in Amos 1 und 2' in *Schalom (Studien zu Glaube und Geschichte Israels, A. Jepsen zum 70. Geburtstag dargebracht)*, ed. K.-H. Bernhardt, Stuttgart 1971, argues that the sin of abandoning the law contains all the other sins with which Amos might have charged Judah, so that this objection does not stand; though he accepts the deletion of v.4b (the condemnation of idols). There are, however, no other examples of such an attitude to 'the Torah' in Amos. Rudolph also denies that the small formal variations noted by Wolff can be used to support deletions, since other variations are ignored - e.g. וְתִצַּתִּי for וְשִׁלַּחְתִּי in 1.14. But it must be said that the allegedly significant variations noted above are more substantial than this.

33 Marti, *op. cit.*

34 B. Duhm, 'Anmerkungen zu den zwölf Propheten', *ZAW* 31 (1911), 1-43 (especially 8-9).

35 Marti, *op. cit.*

36 See above, pp. 12-13.

Chapter 4

1 The dating followed in this chapter is that of K. T. Andersen, 'Die Chronologie der Könige von Israel und Juda', *STh* 23 (1969), 69-114.

2 See Weiser, *Das Buch der zwölf kleinen Propheten*, and cf. J. Bright, *A History of Israel*, London 1966, 252.

3 Clements, *Prophecy and Tradition*, 65.

4 In a private communication.

5 Wolff, *Joel and Amos*, 148-51.

6 Herrmann, *A History of Israel*, part II, chapters 6 and 7.

7 On Aramaean history see E. G. H. Kraeling, *Aram and Israel*, New York 1918; A. Malamat, 'The Arameans' in *Peoples of Old Testament Times*, ed. D. J. Wiseman, and bibliography there.

8 Herrmann, *op cit.*, 213.

9 Reading the verbs in I Kings 11.24 as singular, with Gray, *I & II Kings* (OTL), *ad loc.*

10 See Herrmann, *op. cit.*, 176; Bright, *op cit.*, 193.

11 Bright, *op. cit.*, 224.

12 See Malamat, 'The Arameans'.

13 J. M. Miller, 'The Elisha Cycle and the Accounts of the Omride Wars', *JBL* 85 (1966), 441-54, following A. Jepsen, 'Israel und Damaskus', *AfO* 14 (1942), 153-72, and ultimately A. Kuenen (*Historisch-kritische Einleitung in die Bücher des alten Testaments*, I.2, p. 83 note 13) and

G. Hölscher (*Eucharisterion*, 185–91). Cf. also Miller's 'The Fall of the House of Ahab', *VT* 17 (1967), 307–24. Miller's arguments are summarised in his *The Old Testament and the Historian*, London 1976, chapter 2.

14 See Jepsen, *op. cit.* A common explanation has been that 'Ben-hadad' was a 'throne name': cf. M. Unger, *Israel and the Aramaeans of Damascus*, London 1957, 70, and Kraeling, *op. cit.*, chapter 9.

15 Incidentally this is another argument against supposing that Amos is here selecting from much older oracles, as Kaufmann thinks (*History of the Religion of Israel*, III.1, 61–2); the oracle cannot antedate the accession of the sole Ben-hadad, in the time of Jehu at the earliest.

16 *ANET* 279–80; cf. Malamat, 'The Arameans'.

17 Miller argues (*VT* 17, 313–14, and *JBL* 85, 444–5) that the discrepancy between this passage and I Kings 22 is evidence for the 'double redaction' of the Deuteronomic History rejected by M. Noth in *Überlieferungs-geschichtliche Studien*, I, Halle 1943, especially 45–64. This is too large a question to enter into here.

18 Unless we take seriously the account in II Kings 6 of a siege of Samaria by 'Ben-hadad' in the reign of Joram, a little before this. But see below.

19 Malamat, 'The Arameans', 145. Wolff (*Joel and Amos*, 150) identifies Adad-nirari III with the 'saviour' of II Kings 13.5 (thus also Gottwald, *All the Kingdoms of the Earth*, 82), though Herrmann (*op. cit.*, 228) thinks that this refers to an earlier and very temporary check to the Aramaean advance by an unnamed charismatic leader in Israel itself. There seems little to be said for the Jerusalem Bible's suggestion that Jeroboam II is meant, by anticipation. There have been many other suggested identifications, including Elisha (thus Miller, 'The Elisha Cycle', 442–3). J. A. Soggin ('Amos VI.13–14 und I.3 auf dem Hintergrund der Beziehungen zwischen Israel und Damaskus im 9. und 8. Jahrhundert' in *Near Eastern Studies in Honor of W. F. Albright*, ed. H. Goedicke, Baltimore and London 1971, 433–41) comments ruefully 'quot capita, tot sententiae'.

20 Herrmann, *op. cit.*, 232.

21 This represents a return to the views of Miller's predecessors, such as Jepsen (*op. cit.*).

22 II Kings 6.8–23 represents a separate problem: another account from the days of Ben-hadad, but impossible to date.

23 Compare Gray, *op. cit.*, 404.

24 Haran, 'The Rise and Decline of the Empire of Jeroboam ben Joash', 266–97.

25 On the meaning of 'Lebo-hamath' see K. Elliger, 'Die Nordgrenze des Reiches Davids', *PJB* 32 (1936), 34–73 (especially 42). Haran (*op. cit.*, 282–4) argues that, whatever its exact meaning, the general sense of the stereotyped phrase is that Jeroboam had free access to the Euphrates, i.e. had restored in principle the northern holdings of Solomon.

26 Wolff, *Joel and Amos*, 150.

27 The Sefire treaties provide evidence for the relative independence of the Aramaean states at this time; see Fitzmyer, *The Aramaic Inscriptions of Sefire*, and M. Noth, 'Der historische Hintergrund der Inschriften von sefire', *ZDPV* 77 (1961), 138–45.

28 See Soggin, *op. cit.*

29 S. Cohen, 'The Political Background of the Words of Amos', *HUCA* 36 (1965), 153–60, argues strongly for this: even if Karnaim and Lo-debar are recent *victories*, 4.10f and 5.15 probably point to recent setbacks.

30 Cf. above, p. 20.

31 On סגר see above, p. 20.

32 Kaufmann, *History of the Religion of Israel*, II.1, 61ff.

33 Cf. Gray, *op. cit.*, *ad loc.* For counter-arguments see R. E. Murphy, 'Israel and Moab in the Ninth Century B.C.', *CBQ* 15 (1953), 409–17.

34 K.-H. Bernhardt, 'Der Feldzug der drei Könige' in *Schalom* (Festschrift for A. Jepsen), 11–22.

35 See above, p. 29.

36 Gottwald, *op. cit.*, 70–4, sees this as a 'Holy War'. Even if this is so, it conflicts just as strongly with the presentation of the campaign, in 3.7, as the reconquest of a rebellious vassal.

37 Thus Bartlett, 'The Moabites and Edomites', 238.

38 This was suggested by Wellhausen, though it is dismissed as too speculative by M. Noth, 'Eine palästinische Lokalüberlieferung in 2 Chron. 20' *ZDPV* 67 (1944), 45–71, who prefers to see it as a reminiscence of a small local confrontation much nearer to the Chronicler's day; and by W. Rudolph, *Chronikbücher*, HAT 21, 1955, *ad loc.*

39 It may be noted that the Lucianic recension of the LXX reads 'Ahaziah' for 'Jehoshaphat' in this chapter – see J. R. Bartlett, 'The Rise and Fall of the Kingdom of Edom', *PEQ* 104 (1972), 26–37; cf. also J. D. Shenkel, *Chronology and Recensional Development in the Greek Text of Kings*, Cambridge 1968, 93–108.

Chapter 5

1 Thus Weiser in *Das Buch der zwölf kleinen Propheten* and in *Die Profetie des Amos*, BZAW 53, 1929; Edghill, *The Book of Amos*; J. Marsh, *Amos and Micah*, London 1959; S. Lehming, 'Erwägungen zu Amos', *ZThK* 55 (1958), 145–69; Cripps, *Commentary*; P. Humbert, *Un héraut de la justice – Amos*, Lausanne 1917; J. Vollmer, *Geschichtliche Rückblicke und Motive in der Prophetie des Amos, Hosea und Jesaja*, BZAW 119, 1971; E. Hammershaimb, *The Book of Amos*, Oxford 1970; Wolff, *Joel and Amos*.

2 'Musik für die Ohren der lauschenden Israeliten' (Weiser, *Die Profetie des Amos*, 102).

3 Cf. H. W. Wolff, 'Das Zitat im Prophetenspruch' in *Gesammelte Studien*, Munich 1964, 36–129 (= *EvTh* Beiheft 4 (1937), 3–112).

4 Würthwein, 'Amosstudien'; cf. the same author's 'Der Ursprung der prophetischen Gerichtsrede'.

5 Weiser (*Die Profetie des Amos, 21*) makes a strong case for deliberate dramatic effect here. Much the same point about Yahweh's patience is made in 4.6–12, though there the 'chances' have been provided by awful warnings rather than by acts of obvious mercy.

6 Wolff, 'Das Zitat'.

7 See J. W. Whedbee, *Isaiah and Wisdom*, Nashville 1971, 47.

8 See S. Terrien, 'Amos and Wisdom' in *Israel's Prophetic Heritage*, ed. B. W. Anderson and W. Harrelson, New York 1962; J. Lindblom, 'Wisdom

in the Old Testament Prophets' in *Wisdom in Israel and in the Ancient Near East*, ed. M. Noth, *VTS* 3 (1960); and H. W. Wolff, *Amos' geistige Heimat.*

9   See Wolff's comments, *Joel and Amos*, 312–14.
10 See above, p. 12, for discussion of the view that oracles against the nations imply victory for Israel.
11 Cf. the similar criticisms by Lehming, *op. cit.*
12 See p. 00 above.
13 Kapelrud, *Central Ideas in Amos.*

Chapter 6

1   See above, pp. 11, 37–8.
2   Haran, 'Jeroboam ben Joash', 273–4.
3   This is also the explanation given by Haran.
4   Weiser, *Die Profetie des Amos*, 112.
5   F. C. Fensham, 'Common Trends in Curses of the Near Eastern Treaties and *kudurru*-Inscriptions compared with Maledictions of Amos and Isaiah', *ZAW* 75 (1957), 155–75.
6   R. E. Clements, *Prophecy and Covenant*, SBTh I.43, 1965. Clements's more recent work (*Prophecy and Tradition*) seriously modifies this conclusion.
7   Mays, *Amos* (OTL); cf. Wolff, *Joel and Amos*, 106.
8   Weiser, *Die Profetie des Amos*, 104.
9   Cf. E. Baumann, *Der Aufbau der Amosreden*, BZAW 7, 1903.
10 Cf. Wolff, *Joel and Amos*, 101: 'That Yahweh is the only God of Israel and of the world of nations is not a theme of his message but its self-evident presupposition.'
11 Thus Cramer, *Amos*, 156ff.
12 Cf. Beek, 'The Religious Background', 132, and Nowack, *Die kleinen Propheten.*
13 J. Lindblom, *Prophecy in Ancient Israel*, Oxford 1962, 335 (footnote).
14 Cf. Kapelrud, *Central Ideas in Amos*, 17ff.
15 Humbert, *Un héraut de la justice*, 22 and 27 respectively; cf. also F. Nötscher, *Die Gerechtigkeit Gottes bei den vorexilischen Propheten*, Münster-i.-W. 1915, 79: 'Es ist für Jahwes Strafe nach Amos ohne Belang, ob die Sünden gegen sein Volk gerichtet sind oder nicht; die Verletzung der rechten sittlichen Ordnung an sich ist strafbar.' Cf. *ibid.*, 85: 'Die Schuld der Heiden liegt meist in einer ihnen wohl zurechenbaren Ueberschreitung der rechten Ordnung.'
16 H. S. Gehman, 'Natural Law and the Old Testament' in *Biblical Studies in Memory of H. C. Alleman*, ed. J. M. Myers, O. Reimherr and H. N. Bream, New York 1960, 109–22.
17 *Ibid.*, 113. Cf. Clements, *Prophecy and Tradition*, 65, and the discussion in Jones, 'Some Leading Motifs', 156ff.
18 M. Weber, *Ancient Judaism*, Glencoe, Ill. 1952, 302.
19 Jones, *op. cit.*, 156.

Chapter 7

1   See above, p. 41.

2 Weiser, *Die Profetie des Amos*, 112.
3 E. W. Heaton, *The Hebrew Kingdoms*, Oxford 1968, 266.

Appendix: International law in the ancient Near East

1 W. Preiser, 'Zum Völkerrecht der vorklassischen Antike', *Archiv des Völkerrechts* 4 (1954), 257–88.
2 Cf. T. J. Lawrence, *The Principles of International Law*, London 1895, especially 26; E. von Ullmann, 'Völkerrecht' in *Das öffentliche Recht der Gegenwart*, ed. G. Jellinek *et al.*, vol. 3 (12th edn), Tübingen 1935.
3 Full details in A. Poebel, 'Der Konflikt zwischen Lagas und Umma z. Z. Enannatums I und Entemenas' in *Oriental Studies* (Festschrift for Paul Haupt, Johns Hopkins University), ed. C. Adler and A. Ember, Baltimore 1926, 220–67.
4 Cf. A. Nussbaum, *A Concise History of the Law of Nations*, 2nd edn, New York 1962, 1. There is a possible example of mediation between two *sovereign* states by Zimri-lim in the Mari letters, discussed by J. M. Munn-Rankin in her 'Diplomacy in Western Asia in the Early Second Millennium B.C.', *Iraq* 18 (1956), 68–110 – see especially 78f.
5 Text in E. F. Weidner, *Politische Dokumente aus Kleinasien*, Leipzig 1923, 112–23.
6 W. Mettgenberg, 'Vor mehr als 3000 Jahren – ein Beitrag zur Geschichte des Auslieferungsrechts', *Zeitschrift für Völkerrecht* 23 (1939), 23–32. The existence of extradition treaties may be attested by I Kings 2.39 and 18.10; see K. A. Kitchen, 'The Philistines' in *Peoples of Old Testament Times*, ed. D. J. Wiseman, 65.
7 Sections 17 and 18.
8 D. J. Wiseman, *The Alalakh Tablets*, London 1953, 30.
9 *Ibid.*, 29.
10 *Ibid.*
11 See V. Korošec, *Hethitische Staatsverträge*, Leipziger rechtswissenschaftliche Studien 60, Leipzig 1931.
12 On this point cf. A. Wegner, *Geschichte des Völkerrechts*, Stuttgart 1936; vassal treaties stand 'erst auf der Schwelle der Rechtsgeschichte', when 'weder VR noch Staatsrecht voll ausgebildet sind' (p. 3).
13 Weidner, *op. cit.*, 17ff.
14 Cf. in this connection the letter of accusation from Arnuwandaš to Madduwattaš, which complains that extradition arrangements have been allowed to lapse. See A. Götze, *Madduwattaš*, MVAG 32 (1), 1927, 146–7.
15 Noth ('Der historische Hintergrund') thinks they are in fact one half of a parity treaty.
16 See Fitzmyer, *The Aramaic Inscriptions of Sefire*.
17 *Ibid.*
18 J. Knudtzon, *Die El-Amarna Tafeln*, Leipzig 1907–8 (= *EA*).
19 Munn-Rankin, *op. cit.*.
20 ARMT II. 24.
21 ARMT I. 15.
22 ARMT V. 11.
23 ARMT VI. 15, 7–9.
24 ARMT II. 73.

25 J. Pirenne, 'Le droit international sous la XVIIIe dynastie égyptienne aux XVe et XVIe siècles av. J.-C.', *Revue internationale des droits de l'antiquité* 5 (1958), 3–19.

26 Cf. Munn-Rankin, *op. cit.*, 96–9..

27 *EA* 42. The same order is to be found in the Mari letters.

28 *EA* 34.

29 *EA* 81 and 189.

30 *EA* 55 and 140.

31 *EA* 89, 122 and 123.

32 Deut. 27.17 etc., and all the *kudurru*-inscriptions. Cf. *KAI* 259.

33 *KAI* 1; cf *KAI* 14, also translated in G. A. Cooke, *A Text-Book of North Semitic Inscriptions*, Oxford 1903, 31: *KAI* 9, 13, 79, 191 and 225; Livy, *Ab urbe condita* XXXI. 30.2–7.

34 VTE 545f, cf. 449–50, and see D. J. McCarthy, *Treaty and Covenant*, Rome 1963, 201ff. See also Lev. 26.29; Deut. 28.53ff; II Kings 6.28f; Jer. 19.9; Lam. 2.20, 4.10; Ezek. 5.10.

35 *EA* 74; cf. *EA* 62, 75 and 142.

36 Quoted by Wolff (*Joel and Amos*, 161) from H. Schmökel, *Ur, Assur, und Babylon*, Stuttgart 1955, 114.

37 *Iliad* VI. 57f.

38 The annals of the Assyrian and Neo-Babylonian kings abound in gloating accounts of horrible tortures inflicted on captured enemies and rebellious vassals; and compare some of the scenes in the Nimrud wall reliefs. For a classic series of atrocities see D. D. Luckenbill, *The Annals of Sennacherib*, Chicago 1924, 5f.

39 Thus J. A. Montgomery and H. S. Gehman, *The Books of Kings*, ICC, 1951, *ad loc.*

40 Thus Gray, *I & II Kings* (OTL), 515.

41 II Sam. 3.34 might be of interest here. When David laments that Abner was not fettered or manacled, he is presumably saying first that his murder was an act of treachery, as in the passage just discussed; but there does seem to be a clear implication that those who have been fettered may be killed. But if, as H. W. Hertzberg maintains (*I & II Samuel* OTĹ, 1964, *ad loc.*), the reference is not to an enemy taken in war but to a criminal awaiting execution, the verse is not relevant to our purposes.

42 See A. Götze, *Kleinasien*, 2nd edn, part III.1 of *Kulturgeschichte des alten Orients*, Munich 1957, 122ff, and especially 127. This is my chief source for what follows, but for some discussion of evidence for these points from the original texts see the Additional Note, pp. 60–1.

43 A. Alt, 'Hethitische und ägyptische Herrschaftsordnung in unterworfenen Gebieten' in *Kleine Schriften zur Geschichte des Volkes Israel*, vol. 3, Munich 1953, 99–106 (= *Forschungen und Fortschritte* 25 (1949), 249–51) argues against too great an emphàsis on the humanitarianism of the Hittites; still, the differences from their neighbours are striking.

44 Text and translation in A. Götze, *Die Annalen des Muršiliš*, MVAG 38 (6), 1933. The original publications of the annals are referred to by somewhat complicated abbreviations; see the List of Abbreviations, pp. ix–x above, for their explanation.

45 *Ibid.*, 47; *KBo* III (= 2*BoTU* 48 (II)), 9–14. This is effectively a trial by

battle (see p. 58 above). For a complicated challenge of this sort from Roman times cf. Livy, *Ab urbe condita* I. 32.6-14. The practice of issuing an ultimatum is well attested in the ancient Near East; cf. the Epic of Tukulti-Ninurta, in R. C. Thompson, 'The Excavations on the Temple of Nabu at Nineveh', *Archaeologia* 79 (1929), 126-33 (French translation in J. Harvey, *Le plaidoyer prophétique contre Israël après la rupture de l'alliance*, Studia 22, Bruges 1967); the Indictment of Iarîm-Lim of Alep, Mari letter A1314, in G. Dossin, 'Une lettre de Iarîm-Lim, roi d'Alep, à Iašub-Iahad, roi de Dîr', *Syria* 33 (1956), 63-9; the Ultimatum to Milavata, in F. Sommer, *Die Aḫḫiyava-Urkunden*, Munich 1932, 65-6; and the accusation of Madduwattaš, cited on p. 70 in note 14. And compare Judges 11.12-29.

46 See above, p. 58.

47 *KBo* III 4(= 2*BoTU* 48 (IX)), 43-8 (Götze, *Die Annalen des Muršiliš*, 37); *Bo* II 43 (II), 23; *KBo* III 4 (= 2*BoTU* 48 (II)), 6: *KBo* III 4 (= 2*BoTU* 48 (IV)), 28.

48 *KUB* XIV 15 (= 2*BoTU* 51A), 7-23.

49 *KUB* XIV 15 (= 2*BoTU* 51A), 45-50. See above, p. 58.

50 *KBo* III 4 (= 2*BoTU* 48 (III)), 11-20 (Götze, *Die Annalen des Muršiliš*, 71).

51 *KUB* XIX 37 (= 2*BoTU* 60 III), 41-8. Many more details of the practice of war in the ancient Near East, most of them not directly relevant to our limited purposes, are to be found in *Iraq* 25 (1963), which was devoted to the subject. The points we have made about Hittite rules of war will be found in A. Götze, 'Warfare in Asia Minor' (124-30); and V. Korošec, 'The Warfare of the Hittites – from the Legal Point of View' (159-66). W. von Soden, 'Die Assyrer und der Krieg' (131-44) questions how aggressive the Assyrians really were, and emphasises that the trait becomes apparent only well into the first millennium, though even so he concedes superiority to the Hittites; and H. W. F. Saggs, 'Assyrian Warfare in the Sargonid Period' (145-54) doubts whether they were really exceptional in their brutality. That Hittites were less ferocious than Assyrians has long been a received opinion: see O. Gurney, *The Hittites*, London 1952, 115.

BIBLIOGRAPHY

Albright, W. F. 'The Oracles of Balaam', *JBL* 63 (1944), 207-33.
Alt, A.'Hethitische und ägyptische Herrschaftsordnung in unterworfenen Gebieten'
in *Kleine Schriften zur Geschichte des Volkes Israel*, vol. 3, Munich 1953,
99-106 (= *Forschungen und Fortschritte* 25 (1949), 249-51).
Andersen, K. T. 'Die Chronologie der Könige von Israel und Juda', *STh* 23 (1969),
69-114.
Bach, R. *Die Aufforderung zur Flucht und zum Kampf im alttestamentlichen Prophe-
tenspruch*, WMANT 9, Neukirchen 1962.
Bartlett, J. R. 'The Moabites and Edomites' in *Peoples of Old Testament Times*, ed.
D. J. Wiseman, Oxford 1973, 228-58.
'The Rise and Fall of the Kingdom of Edom', *PEQ* 104 (1972), 26-37.
Baumann, E. *Der Aufbau der Amosreden*, BZAW 7, Berlin 1903.
Beek, M. A. 'The Religious Background of Amos 2.6-8', *OS* 5 (1948), 132-41.
Begrich, J. 'Das priesterliche Heilsorakel', *ZAW* 52 (1934), 81-92.
Bentzen, A. 'The Ritual Background of Amos 1.2-2.16', *OS* 8 (1950), 85-99.
Bernhardt, K.-H. 'Der Feldzug der drei Könige' in *Schalom (Studien zu Glaube und
Geschichte Israels, A. Jepsen zum 70. Geburtstag dargebracht)*, ed. K.-H.
Bernhardt, Stuttgart 1971, 11-22.
Bright, J. *A History of Israel*, London 1966.
Budde, K. 'Zu Text und Auslegung des Buches Amos', *JBL* 43 (1924), 46-131.
Childs, B. S. *Isaiah and the Assyrian Crisis*, SBTh II.3, London 1967.
Clements, R. E. *Prophecy and Covenant*, SBTh I.43, London 1965.
Prophecy and Tradition, Oxford 1975.
Cohen, S. 'The Political Background of the Words of Amos', *HUCA* 36 (1965),
153-60.
Cooke, G. A. *A Text-Book of North Semitic Inscriptions*, Oxford 1903.
Cramer, K. *Amos - Versuch einer theologischen Interpretation*, BWANT III.15,
Leipzig 1930.
Cripps, R. S. *A Critical and Exegetical Commentary on the Book of Amos*,
2nd edn, London 1955.
Cross, F. M. and Freedman, D. N. 'The Blessing of Moses', *JBL* 67 (1948), 191-210.
Dossin, G. 'Une lettre de Iarîm-Lim, roi d'Alep, à Iašub-Iahad, roi de Dîr', *Syria* 33
(1956), 63-9.
'Sur le prophétisme à Mari' in *La divination en Mésopotamie ancienne et dans les
régions voisines* (14e rencontre assyriologique internationale, Strasbourg
2-6 July 1965), Paris 1966, 77-86.

Driver, G. R. 'Linguistic and Textual Problems – Minor Prophets II' *JTS* 39 (1938), 260–73.

Duhm, B. 'Anmerkungen zu den zwölf Propheten', *ZAW* 31 (1911), 1–43.

Edghill, E. A. *The Book of Amos*, London 1914.

Ellermeier, F. *Prophetie in Mari und Israel*, Theologische und orientalische Arbeiten 1, Hertzberg 1968.

Elliger, K. 'Die Nordgrenze des Reiches Davids', *PJB* 32 (1936), 34–73.

Fensham, F. C. 'Common Trends in Curses of the Near Eastern Treaties and *kudurru-*Inscriptions compared with Maledictions of Amos and Isaiah', *ZAW* 75 (1957), 155–75.

Fishbane, M. 'Additional Remarks on RHMYW (Amos 1.11)', *JBL* 91 (1972), 391–3.
'The Treaty Background of Amos 1.11', *JBL* 89 (1970), 313–18.

Fitzmyer, J. A. *The Aramaic Inscriptions of Sefire*, Biblica et Orientalia 19, Rome 1967.

Fohrer, G. 'Prophetie und Magie' in *Studien zur alttestamentlichen Prophetie (1949–65)*, BZAW 99, Berlin 1967, 242–64 (reprinted from *ZAW* 78 (1966)).
'Remarks on Modern Interpretations of the Prophets', *JBL* 80 (1961), 309–19.

Fosbroke, H. E. W. *Amos*, IB VI, New York 1956.

Gehman, H. S. 'Natural Law and the Old Testament' in *Biblical Studies in Memory of H. C. Alleman*, ed. J. M. Myers, O. Reimherr and H. N. Bream, New York 1960, 109–22.

Gottwald, N. K. *All the Kingdoms of the Earth*, New York and London 1964.

Götze, A. *Die Annalen des Muršiliš*, MVAG 38 (6), Leipzig 1933.
Kleinasien 2nd edn, part III.1 of *Kulturgeschichte des alten Orients*, Munich 1957.
Madduwattaš, MVAG 32 (1), Leipzig 1927.
'Warfare in Asia Minor', *Iraq* 25 (1963), 124–30.

Gray, J. *I & II Kings*, OTL, London 1964.

Gurney, O. *The Hittites*, London 1952.

Hammershaimb, E. *The Book of Amos*, Oxford 1970.

Haran, M. 'The Rise and Decline of the Empire of Jeroboam ben Joash', *VT* 17 (1967), 266–97.

Harper, W. R. *Amos and Hosea*, ICC, Edinburgh 1905.

Harvey, J. *Le plaidoyer prophétique contre Israël après la rupture de l'alliance*, Studia 22, Bruges 1967.

Hayes, J. H. 'Prophetism at Mari and Old Testament Parallels', *AThR* 49 (1967), 397–409.
'The Usage of Oracles against Foreign Nations in Ancient Israel', *JBL* 87 (1968), 81–92.

Heaton, E. W. *The Hebrew Kingdoms*, Oxford 1968.

Helck, W. *Die Beziehungen Ägyptens zu Vorderasien im 3. und 2. Jahrtausend vor Chr.*, Ägyptologische Abhandlungen 5, Wiesbaden 1962.

Herrmann, S. *A History of Israel in Old Testament Times*, London 1975.

Hertzberg, H. W. *I & II Samuel*, OTL, London 1964.

Hogg, H. W. 'The Starting Point of the Religious Message of Amos' in *Transactions of the 3rd International Congress for the History of Religions*, ed. P. S. Allen and J. de M. Johnson, Oxford 1908, I.325–7.

Hölscher, G. *Eucharisterion* (Festschrift for H. Gunkel), Göttingen 1923.

Humbert, P. *Un héraut de la justice – Amos*, Lausanne 1917.

Jepsen, A. 'Israel und Damaskus', *AfO* 14 (1942), 153–72.

Jones, G. H. 'An Examination of Some Leading Motifs in the Prophetic Oracles against Foreign Nations', PhD. Diss (unpublished), University College of North Wales, Bangor, 1970.

Kapelrud, A. S. *Central Ideas in Amos*, Oslo 1961.

Kaufmann, Y. *A History of the Religion of Israel* (tr. M. Greenberg), London 1961.

Kitchen, K. A. 'The Philistines' in *Peoples of Old Testament Times*, ed. D. J. Wiseman, Oxford 1973, 53–78.

Knudtzon, J. *Die El-Amarna Tafeln*, Leipzig 1907–8.

Korošec, V. *Hethitische Staatsverträge*, Leipziger rechtswissenschaftliche Studien 60, Leipzig 1931.

'The Warfare of the Hittites – from the Legal Point of View', *Iraq* 25 (1963), 159–66.

Kraeling, E. G. H. *Aram and Israel*, New York 1918.

Kraus, H. J. *Psalmen*, BK XV, Neukirchen 1966.

Kuenen, A. *Historisch-kritische Einleitung in die Bücher des alten Testaments*, 3 vols., Leipzig 1885–94.

Lawrence, T. J. *The Principles of International Law*, London 1895.

Lehming, S. 'Erwägungen zu Amos', *ZThK* 55 (1958), 145–69.

Lindblom, J. *Prophecy in Ancient Israel*, Oxford 1962.

'Wisdom in the Old Testament Prophets' in *Wisdom in Israel and in the Ancient Near East*, ed. M. Noth, *VTS* 3 (1960).

Luckenbill, D. D. *The Annals of Sennacherib*, Chicago 1924.

Maag, V. *Text, Wortschatz und Begriffswelt des Buches Amos*, Leiden 1951.

McCarthy, D. J. *Treaty and Covenant*, Rome 1963.

Macpherson, C. B. *The Political Theory of Possessive Individualism*, Oxford 1962.

Malamat, A. 'Amos 1.5 in the Light of the Til Barsip Inscriptions', *BASOR* 129 (1953), 25f.

'The Arameans' in *Peoples of Old Testament Times*, ed. D. J. Wiseman, Oxford 1973, 134–55.

'Prophetic Revelations in New Documents from Mari and the Bible', *VTS* 15 (1966), 214–19.

Marsh, J. *Amos and Micah*, London 1959.

Marti, K. 'Zur Komposition von Amos 1.3–2.3', BZAW 33, Berlin 1917, 323–30.

Mays, J. L. *Amos*, OTL, London 1969.

Mettgenberg, W. 'Vor mehr als 3000 Jahren – ein Beitrag zur Geschichte des Auslieferungsrechts', *Zeitschrift für Völkerrecht* 23 (1939), 23–32.

Miller, J. M. 'The Elisha Cycle and the Accounts of the Omride Wars', *JBL* 85 (1966), 441–54.

'The Fall of the House of Ahab', *VT* 17 (1967), 307–24.

The Old Testament and the Historian, London 1976.

Montgomery, J. A. and Gehman, H. S. *The Books of Kings*, ICC, Edinburgh 1951.

Moran, W. L. 'New Evidence from Mari on the History of Prophecy', *Biblica* 50 (1969), 15–56.

Morgenstern, J. 'Amos Studies IV', *HUCA* 32 (1961).

Mowinckel, S. *The Psalms in Israel's Worship*, Oxford 1962.

Munn-Rankin, J. M. 'Diplomacy in Western Asia in the Early Second Millennium B.C.', *Iraq* 18 (1956), 68–110.

Murphy, R. E. 'Israel and Moab in the Ninth Century B.C.', *CBQ* 15 (1953), 409–17.

Néher, A. *Amos*, Paris 1950.

Noth, M. 'Der historische Hintergrund der Inschriften von sefire', *ZDPV* 77 (1961), 138–45.

'Eine palästinische Lokalüberlieferung in 2 Chron. 20', *ZDPV* 67 (1944), 45–71.

Überlieferungsgeschichtliche Studien, Halle 1943.

Nötscher, F. *Die Gerechtigkeit Gottes bei den vorexilischen Propheten*, Münster-i.-W. 1915.

Nowack, W. *Die kleinen Propheten*, Göttingen 1897.

Nussbaum, A. *A Concise History of the Law of Nations*, 2nd edn, New York 1962.

Paul, S. M. 'Amos 1.3–2.3: A Concatenous Literary Pattern', *JBL* 90 (1971), 397–403.

Pirenne, J. 'Le droit international sous la XVIIIe dynastie égyptienne aux XVe et XVIe siècles av. J.-C.', *Revue internationale des droits de l'antiquité* 5 (1958), 3–19.

Poebel, A. 'Der Konflikt zwischen Lagas und Umma z. Z. Enannatums I und Entemenas' in *Oriental Studies* (Festschrift for Paul Haupt, Johns Hopkins University), ed. C. Adler and A. Ember, Baltimore 1926, 220–67.

Preiser, W. 'Zum Völkerrecht der vorklassischen Antike', *Archiv des Völkerrechts* 4 (1954), 257–88.

Priest, J. 'The Covenant of Brothers', *JBL* 84 (1965), 400–6.

Rad, G. von. *Der heilige Krieg im alten Israel*, Zurich 1951.

Old Testament Theology, London 1965.

Reventlow, H. Graf. *Das Amt des Propheten bei Amos*, Göttingen 1962.

Liturgie und prophetisches Ich bei Jeremia, Gütersloh 1963.

Wächter Über Israel. Ezechiel und seine Traditionen, BZAW 82, Berlin 1962.

Robinson, T. H. *Die zwölf kleinen Propheten*, HAT, Tübingen 1938.

Roth, W. M. W. 'Numerical Sayings in the Old Testament', *VTS* 13 (1965).

'The Numerical Sequence x/x + 1 in the Old Testament', *VT* 12 (1962), 300–11.

Rudolph, W. 'Die angefochtenen Völkersprüche in Amos 1 und 2, in *Schalom (Studien zu Glaube und Geschichte Israels, A. Jepsen zum 70. Geburtstag dargebracht)*, ed. K.-H. Bernhardt, Stuttgart 1971.

Chronikbücher, HAT 21, Tübingen 1955.

Saggs, H. W. F. 'Assyrian Warfare in the Sargonid Period', *Iraq* 25 (1963), 145–54.

Schmökel, H. *Ur, Assur, und Babylon*, Stuttgart 1955.

Schmuttermayr, G. 'RḤM – eine lexikalische Studie', *Biblica* 51 (1970), 499–532.

Shenkel, J. D. *Chronology and Recensional Development in the Greek Text of Kings*, Cambridge 1968.

Soden, W. von. 'Die Assyrer und der Krieg', *Iraq* 25 (1963), 131–44.

Soggin, J. A. 'Amos VI.13–14 und I.3 auf dem Hintergrund der Beziehungen zwischen Israel und Damaskus im 9. und 8. Jahrhundert' in *Near Eastern Studies in Honor of W. F. Albright*, ed. H. Goedicke, Baltimore and London 1971, 433–41.

Sommer, F. *Die Aḫḫiyava-Urkunden*, Munich 1932.

Stolz, F. *Interpreting the Old Testament*, London 1975.

Tallquist, K. *Himmelsgegenden und Winde*, Studia Orientalia 2, Helsinki 1928.

Terrien, S. 'Amos and Wisdom' in *Israel's Prophetic Heritage*, ed. B. W. Anderson and W. Harrelson, New York 1962.

Thompson, R. C. 'The Excavations on the Temple of Nabu at Nineveh', *Archaeologia* 79 (1929).

Torczyner, N. H. *hallason w^e hassepher*, Jerusalem 1955.

Ullmann, E. von. 'Völkerrecht' in *Das öffentliche Recht der Gegenwart*, ed. G. Jellinek *et al.*, vol. 3, 12th edn, Tübingen 1935.

Unger, M. *Israel and the Aramaeans of Damascus*, London 1957.

Vaux, R. de. 'Single Combat in the Old Testament' in *The Bible and the Ancient Near East*, London 1972, 122-35.

Vollmer, J. *Geschichtliche Rückblicke und Motive in der Prophetie des Amos, Hosea und Jesaja*, BZAW 119, Berlin 1971.

Waldow, E. von. *Der traditionsgeschichtliche Hintergrund der prophetischen Gerichtsreden*, BZAW 85, Berlin 1963.

Weber, M. *Ancient Judaism*, Glencoe, Ill. 1952.

Wegner, A. *Geschichte des Völkerrechts*, Stuttgart 1936.

Weidner, E. F. *Politische Dokumente aus Kleinasien*, Leipzig 1923.

Weiser, A. *Das Buch der zwölf kleinen Propheten*, ATD, Göttingen 1967.
Die Profetie des Amos, BZAW 53, Berlin 1929.

Weiss, M. 'The Pattern of the "Execration Texts" in the Prophetic Literature', *IEJ* 19 (1969), 150-7.

Whedbee, J. W. *Isaiah and Wisdom*, Nashville 1971.

Wildberger, H. '"Glauben" im Alten Testament', *ZThK* 65 (1968), 129-59.

Wiseman, D. J. *The Alalakh Tablets*, London 1953.
(ed.) *Peoples of Old Testament Times*, Oxford 1973.

Wolff, H. W. *Amos' geistige Heimat*, Neukirchen 1964.
Joel and Amos, Philadelphia 1977 (a translation of *Dodekapropheton 2: Joel und Amos*, BK XIV, Neukirchen 1969).
'Das Zitat im Prophetenspruch' in *Gesammelte Studien*, Munich 1964, 36-129 (= *EvTh* Beiheft 4 (1937), 3-112).

Würthwein, E. 'Amosstudien', *ZAW* 62 (1949), 10-52.
'Jesaja 7, 1-9. Ein Beitrag zu dem Thema "Prophetie und Politik"' in *Theologie als Glaubenswagnis* (Festschrift for Karl Heim), Tübingen and Hamburg 1954, 47-63.
'Der Ursprung der prophetischen Gerichtsrede' in *Wort und Existenz: Studien zum alten Testament*, Göttingen 1970, 111-28 (= *ZThK* 49 (1952), 1-16).

INDEX OF BIBLICAL REFERENCES

INDEX OF AUTHORS CITED